SNOW DAY

SNOW DAY

LESSONS IN LEADERSHIP AND RESILIENCE FROM CRISIS & MASS CASUALTY EVENTS

MARK MCCOURT

Library of Congress Control Number: 2021911475
ISBN: Hardcover   978-1-6641-7881-6
                Softcover   978-1-6641-7880-9
                eBook   978-1-6641-7879-3

Print information available on the last page.

Rev. date: 06/11/2021

To order additional copies of this book, contact:
Xlibris
844-714-8691
www.Xlibris.com
Orders@Xlibris.com
825903

CONTENTS

FOREWORD

"AN INFLEXIBLE BASTARD"

Several decades ago, in the wake of intense geopolitical and terrorist-driven tensions in Indonesia, our company withdrew completely from the country, offending so severely the sensitivities of the Indonesian government that a return years later was initially foreclosed. "You abandoned us in our hour of crisis. Why would we let you back in?" With those wounds, "that hadn't yet felt a scar," still freshly in mind, we received intelligence, post-9/11, that our company interests in Riyadh, Saudi Arabia, were being targeted by Al-Qaida. The bulk of our employees lived in the Al Hamra Oasis Village, a walled community that housed hundreds of employees and their families and was protected by a relatively small team of Pakistani expats.

Our first action was to validate the intelligence, which came to us from the US State Department. When queried, they declared they could only read to us what was "below the tear line"—a signal to me that the original source was the CIA. We reached out to my former colleagues within the CIA for more information and established that the source was reliable HUMINT or SIGINT (human intelligence / signal intelligence). Any possibility of pushing information back upstream that would influence or dissuade the targeting was ruled out. Having established that the threat was "clear and present" and based on a reliable source, I approached our leadership. While acknowledging that "possibilities do not probabilities make" and that probabilities do not themselves rise to the level of "actualities," this intelligence was reliable enough to safely say that it was "not if, but when" our interests would be attacked. I stressed that losing assets that can be replaced is one thing—the loss of human life another. In deference to the "misstep" taken in Indonesia, I recommended the mandatory and immediate repatriation of all "trailing spouses and dependents" and the "voluntary" repatriation of employees not wishing to remain once apprised of the threat. The leadership accepted my recommendation. The order was not open to discussion. A German couple complained that it was "only you Americans that the terrorist hate!" I explained that even a "smart bomb" cannot discriminate based on nationality.

Around 11:15 p.m., on May 12, 2003, a two-vehicle attack team (a sedan loaded with multiple gunmen and a trailing SUV loaded with ANFO [ammonium nitrate/fuel oil]) infiltrated the Al Hamra Oasis Village. Although bolstered and on alert, the guards at the gate were killed in a brief but intense firefight. The terrorists proceeded to open fire at residences. The loss of human life would have been even greater but for the intensity of the blast that occurred when the trailing SOV detonated, taking out the sedan of armed gunmen and leaving a crater twenty feet wide and six feet deep. After the dust settled, we discovered amazingly that, although some required medical treatment, none of our employees had perished. The team continued to meet our contractual obligations to the Saudis without interruption.

Following the May 12 attack, we pulled all our employees from around the city into one heavily fortified compound with .50 caliber machine guns out front and concertina wire on the walls. A British employee living in a compound owned by the Saudi royal family declared that he did not want to live amongst the Americans. That we were going to get him killed. My response—that he would move or be sent home—elicited an unambiguous response from him that I was "an inflexible bastard." He begrudgingly sublet his apartment to a young couple and moved behind the wire. A few weeks later, the compound, owned by the royal family, was also attacked. The young couple to whom he had sublet perished in the attack. The next day, our British employee sent an email to our CEO: "Every day I live, every breath I take from this day forward . . . I owe to that 'inflexible bastard.'" I appreciated that it could well have gone the other way, and on any given day in a war zone, "it's better to be lucky than good."

Snow Day reveals the similar experiences in which the complexities and challenges of making "the right call" in a timely fashion are chronicled. It explores the crisis management programs and decision authority for declaring a crisis, from business disruptions to mass casualty events. Case studies include 9/11 evacuation and non-evacuation decisions that were unevenly decided and/or communicated; nearly identical NYC and LA school district terror threats resulting in different analysis, synthesis, and decisions; and an actual snow day in Atlanta, which left thousands of school students stranded in schools and in buses on roadways. In each of these events, the extent to which crisis management strategy, technology, and communications planning and leadership were leveraged—or not—made all the difference. The pandemic is the mother of all snow days, and the book focuses on interviews with CSOs, risk and resilience experts who share what has been their experience during this crisis. *Snow Day* is a somber reminder to us all of what is at stake in these perilous times and a welcome guide as to how we might best survive them.

John McClurg
Asilomonte
Provo, Utah
March 2021

May 12th 2003 - Riyadh, Saudi Arabia

CHAPTER 1

PROLOGUE: SNOW DAYS, THE 1960s

At an elementary school age, many years ago in Springfield, New Jersey, I rose earlier than necessary on hopeful winter days to perch at our living room window and inspect the falling snow. The brown/green grass of winter slowly whitened, and the asphalt of North View Terrace first fought and melted the snow. Eventually, the snow chilled the lawn and pavement, stuck, and a smooth white landscape of endless playtime possibilities emerged.

Anticipation mixed with impatience grew for that unknown volunteer mom to call the five moms on her list. One mom's phone number was mine. And after a brief call and acknowledgment, my mom would call the five moms on her list. And so on. And an otherwise routine school day would be transformed into a snow day. Sleds and snowball fights displaced memorizing multiplication tables and spelling. A *snow day* had been ordered.

I think back to those days because the same mysteries of my childhood confound risk and critical event planning today. What all-powerful and benevolent person entered my friends' and my small world with such result (and with the same stroke of dialing disrupt our moms' plans). Schools did not open, buses did not roll, and teachers did not drive. Snowplows and children hit the streets with purpose.

But who decided it was a SNOW DAY?

What was the criteria? What information sources were available and relied upon? Who analyzed the information and reached a decision? What preapproved policies were referenced and followed? Was it an individual or a committee? What if they weren't sure? Where did the authority, courage, and experience combine to make the on-time decision to announce a snow day reside?

And what if they (whoever they were) were wrong?

We lived in the era of rotary phones, seven TV channels (including PBS), and turntables (that played 45 RPM records [google it]). And while New York radio's 1010 WINS NEWS reliably broadcast the weather in Central Park every twenty minutes, there was not yet a dedicated weather channel, Weather.com, or smart phones on which to download an app delivering weather by zip code with continuous updated forecasts. (And conversely, if those declaring a snow day were wrong, then no one had access to better information to call them out.)

Looking back, logically the school administration used the available weather information sources to reach a decision. When would the storm begin? How long would it last? How severe might it become? "Good old know-how" from experience and expertise was applied to the data, creating insights about how icy the roads would become and the weather's impact on bus transportation and the ability of teachers and staff to drive.

Certainly, time was also a factor. From the first morning weather and traffic reports to the go-no-go deadline was short but also accurate. Deciding to announce a snow day at 5:00 a.m. based on a weather forecast for 6:00 a.m. had a high probability of being correct (and less probability for being second-guessed).

Having current information and being in proximity to the storm are highly valuable to those analyzing the situation. More challenging is deciding whether or not a snow day should be announced at 5:00 a.m. based on the forecast for the end of the school day. As timelines lengthen and variables increase, the complexity increases and reduces the probability of accurate decision-making. The accuracy of weather information available at 5:00 a.m. about snow accumulation, storm intensity, and road conditions anticipated at 3:00 p.m. creates a lower confidence level.

Why was four inches of snow at 5:00 a.m. not enough to cancel school some days but more than enough on other days? Maybe it was driven by the best guess of the storm's progress and impact during and after the school day. And that information has to be considered in concert with the personal risk tolerance and authority of the snow day's decision-maker.

What do snow days from the 1960s, you ask, have to do with strategic and successful risk management and life safety programs today? Everything. Snow day is a metaphor that meets the constructs of risk management, predicting for and mitigating known events (such as a coming storm) and resilience against unforeseen emergencies that require quick information gathering, analysis, and changes to response.

While my childhood snow days were long ago, the ability to accurately predict and manage current snow days is still a significant challenge for most enterprises, governments, and school systems. And the consequences have proven to be far worse than a child's snow-filled walk to school.

> *You only learn if your emergency preparedness plan works during the actual emergency. All the planning and practicing in the world does not guarantee the plan will work.* (David Shepherd, CEO, Readiness Resource Group)

Much has been learned and applied to better prepare for and respond to snow days. As examples, both the events and the responses during COVID-19, 9/11, Atlanta's actual snow day, and the LA and NYC school terrorism threats highlight how the people, policies, and technologies worked or failed. And how decision-authority has life-and-death consequences.

Crises are incredibly challenging for those charged with gathering, analyzing, deciding, and communicating appropriate action. The policies, people, and technology are relied upon for one purpose: *Get the right information to the right people at the right time to make the right decision to prevent an event from occurring or to properly respond to an event that has occurred, thereby containing a disaster before it becomes a catastrophe.*

Snow Day shares the stories, vision, and expertise of leading resilience and risk management executives who have led business transformation in their enterprises, moving their organizations and stakeholders to a predictive risk management posture, so everyone will be ready and prepared before the storm arrives and not waiting for their mom's rotary phone to ring.

> *Security is always seen as too much until the day it's not enough.* (William Webster, judge and former FBI director and CIA director)

I. FROM CRITICAL TO CATASTROPHIC

CHAPTER 2

A Tale of Two Policies

Jim Dwyer reported in the *New York Times* article "9/11 Tape Has Late Change on Evacuation" (May 17, 2004) that the decision to not immediately evacuate the South Tower resulted in the deaths of over six hundred people. These article excerpts offer insight to the information and decision challenges faced during the chaos created by the terror attacks in New York City.

The first response to the attack came from civilian officials working as deputy fire safety directors in each World Trade Center lobby. After the first plane struck, one director in the South Tower is recorded saying he would not order an evacuation unless the Fire Department or other authority gave the order:

> *I'm not going to do anything until we get orders from the*
> *Fire Department or somebody.*

Over the following fourteen minutes, there were announcements that the South Tower building was secure. And some of the survivors were told to return to their desks. Others were sent to the cafeteria. At nine twelve, just thirteen minutes after the North Tower was hit, a complete evacuation of both towers was called by Port Authority Police Captain Anthony R.

Whitaker. It is not known if that evacuation order reached the lobby desks or was acted upon.

> *The 9/11 terrorist attack on the World Trade Center created chaos, overwhelmed communications systems and left emergency responders with mis- or inadequate information. During hearings by the independent commission investigating the attacks, Jim Dwyer reported that the hearing included "public-address announcements made by an official in the south tower urging tenants to stay in the building even though fire was raging in the other tower."*

The magnitude of the 9/11 attack overwhelmed policies and procedures that were in place. And it exposed the lack of crisis management planning and training. That lack of a planned response and communication in the first moments of the attack resulted in additional deaths.

Martha T. Moore and Dennis Cauchon wrote in *USA Today*, "Delay Meant Death on 9/11," on April 4, 2002, explaining how the decision and information delays to evacuate cost the lives of six hundred people.

> *The people on the top floors of the south tower still had the chance to run, and for them, delay meant death. They had just 16½ minutes before a second jet, United Airlines Flight 175, would tear through the 78th through 84th floors of their building. In that brief window of time, 2,000 people from those floors and up faced a critical choice: stay or go. They didn't know what was coming, but if they moved quickly enough, they survived. Fourteen hundred people fled from the top floors of the south tower to the safe zone below the 78th floor. Six hundred did not.*

Deciding what the policy should be during an emergency is not only too late, it may result in a catastrophic outcome. On 9/11, a very different outcome occurred for Morgan Stanley employees at the World Trade Center, thanks to the foresight, planning, and sacrifice of security chief Rick Rescorla. Assessing (correctly) that the World Trade Center was a terrorist target by predicting the 1993 attack (in 1992), he proposed Morgan

Stanley leave Manhattan and relocate to New Jersey. His proposal was rejected, but he was given authority to create and hold evacuation drills with all employees every three months. He became recognizable as he held a bullhorn during the drills. On September 11, Rescorla ignored the building official's instructions to stay put and began the highly rehearsed and orderly evacuation of Morgan Stanley's 3,700 employees in Tower 2 and 1,000 employees in WTC 5. With bullhorn, policy, and authority in his hands, all 3,700 employees had exited the tower by 9:03 a.m. when United Airline flight 175 hit tower 2.

Rescorla, bullhorn in hand, said he would evacuate "as soon as I make sure everyone else is out" and then turned around and was last seen on the tenth floor, moving upward. Of the six Morgan Stanley employees who died in the attacks, four were Rick Rescorla and three of his security deputies who followed him back into the tower.

With policy and decision-making authority in place, Rick Rescorla was prepared and authorized to call a snow day, saving over 4,700 lives. The lack of policy and authority led to the deaths of over six hundred told to stay at their desks and not evacuate.

As the 9/11 Commission Report stated, the responders exhibited steady determination and resolve under horrifying, overwhelming conditions on 9/11. Effective communications were hampered by command and control and in internal communications, and that cost the lives of those in the buildings. Communicating a planned response, changes in the crisis and its theater, and making decisions that invoke action were not in place for 9/11. The attack was never foreseen as a risk, and therefore no extraordinary plans to mitigate it were in place.

Much has been learned about responding to emergency events from 9/11. The Federal Government changed the way it managed risk and organized emergency services and law enforcement through the Department of Homeland Security. The country's risk posture improved dramatically, and a terrorist attack of 9/11's magnitude has not been repeated. Communication protocols and the policies regarding evacuation and shelter-in-place decisions were reexamined and improved within New York City. Evacuation policies and procedures shifted from a shelter in place (which directed people to stay in the towers) to an evacuation model.

CHAPTER 3

A ZOMBIE APOCALYPSE SNOW DAY

In 2014, Atlanta was no better at predicting and declaring a snow day than 1967 Springfield, New Jersey. Over two thousand students spent the night in schools around the Atlanta area while vehicles were stuck overnight on roads. In some cases, for two nights. Authorities found themselves defending, and in some cases apologizing, for the slow response.

As CBS News reported in "Road to Nowhere: Minor Snowstorm Brings Atlanta to Standstill" on January 29, 2014, there were over 1,200 automotive accidents. At midnight, ninety-nine school buses filled with children were still out, stuck on the roads.

Who gets to call a snow day in Atlanta? Well, it seems everyone and maybe no one. Georgia governor Nathan Deal ordered state workers home on Tuesday afternoon as the weather deteriorated but stated he had no control over what businesses and schools decided to do. The National Guard was called to distribute food and blankets. While Atlanta mayor Kasim Reed pointed out that the interstates are the responsibility of the state government and not the city. And Governor Deal also blamed the forecasters because they led him to believe the storm "would not be so bad."

> *"It looked like the zombie apocalypse," state Rep. Mack Butler said Wednesday. He was driving to a meeting of the Legislature on Tuesday when he had to stop at a gas station in Birmingham and spent the night in his pickup truck because highways were impassable.*

Yet it was Atlanta, home to major corporations and the world's busiest airport, that was Exhibit A for how a Southern city could be sent reeling by winter weather that, in the North, might be no more than an inconvenience. The mayor admitted the city could have directed schools, businesses and government offices to stagger their closings.

Flurries began before noon Tuesday. Ice soon followed. Schools, businesses and government offices closed early— and at nearly the same time. In less than an hour, traffic went from 20 mph to a standstill. Salt and sand trucks could not get through to treat the roads.

Policies, people, and technologies should have been integrated to improve situational awareness and communicate actions more effectively during any emergency, including this actual snow day. But thirteen people died as a result of the storm and the failure to effectively manage the event.

Overall, about two and a half inches of snow fell.

CHAPTER 4

A TALE OF TWO TIME ZONES

The nation's two largest school systems confronted threats of a terrorist attack on Tuesday and reacted in sharply different ways: New York City reviewed the warning and dismissed it as a hoax, but officials here (Los Angeles) abruptly shut down all public schools, upending the lives of parents, students and teachers. (Adam Nagourney, Richard Perez-Pena, and J. David Goodman, "Los Angeles and New York Differ in Their Responses to a Terrorism Threat," *New York Times,* December 15, 2015)

A very different snow day decision faced the leaders in New York City and Los Angeles when an email threatened that some number of jihadists (32 in Los Angeles and 138 in New York City) were ready to attack their schools using bombs, nerve gas, and rifles. Los Angeles has 1,100 schools serving over 640,000 students across a 720 square mile area. New York City has 1,800 schools serving over 1,100,000 students across 469 square miles among its five boroughs.

On December 15, 2015, New York City explained their schools remained open because the threat was clearly a hoax. Los Angeles City explained they closed the school because the threat was credible.

Who decided it was or was not a snow day for their respective districts and based on what criteria?

In Los Angeles, it was school chancellor Ramon C. Cortines.

In New York City, police commissioner William J. Bratton was credited with concluding the threat was not credible. How the final decision was reached to keep the schools open is not clear, but it appears to have been by committee and not a single decision-maker. It is important to note that the threats each received and analyzed were highly similar.

In New York City, one school district superintendent received the threatening email; and upon review by authorities, it was deemed a hoax. Police Chief Bill Bratton stated it was not credible for a number of reasons. And Mayor Bill de Blasio supported the decision, stating, "It would be a disservice to our nation to close down our school system." It is not clear how closing the New York City schools would have had been a disservice to the entire nation.

In Los Angeles, several school board members received the threatening email, and it was reviewed with police. Concluding the threat was credible and choosing caution, Los Angeles school chancellor Ramon C. Cortines announced the districtwide closing. In part, because the horrific shootings in nearby San Bernardino had occurred less than two weeks earlier. Los Angeles mayor Eric Garcetti noted it was not his decision to make, but his to support.

Important is the decision-making process that resulted when each city received and reviewed the threat. In Los Angeles, multiple school board members received the email, and it was reviewed with authorities at 10:00 p.m. Pacific time, Monday, December 14. Los Angeles authorities had the time window to not only close the schools, but get the word out to the press and through social media to students, parents, teachers, administrative employees, school bus operators, law enforcement, and others. Despite this, about one thousand students, teachers, and other employees had not heard about the closing and arrived at closed schools the morning of the fifteenth.

In New York City, the school superintendent who received the email did not read it until 5:00 a.m. Eastern time. The opportunity to put an effective closing plan in motion may have held more risk for their stakeholders than reacting to a non-credible threat.

The New York City Department of Education, "Procedures for School Closings in the Case of Emergency Conditions" states the deputy chancellor of operations decides it is a snow day—after consulting four other city offices and has to do so by 5:00 a.m.:

> *The Chancellor or Deputy Chancellor of Operations will announce the Citywide decision to close schools (including the cancellation of after-school activities) on days of inclement weather or other Citywide emergency*

conditions after consultation with the Mayor's Office of Emergency Management, the Weather Bureau, the City Sanitation Department, the City Transit Authority and other appropriate agencies. The Citywide decision will be made as early as possible prior to 5:00 a.m. on the affected day.

Interestingly, the policy does not include consulting with the chief of police in deciding to close the city's schools. But Police Chief Bill Bratton made the final decision to keep the schools open.

Ultimately, the three-hour time difference drove the different decisions. In Los Angeles, at 10:00 p.m. Pacific time, people were awake, and some were still looking at email. In New York City at 1:00 a.m. Eastern time, the intended recipient was not reading emails. Los Angeles had over seven hours to decide and act. New York City already missed its policy deadline to decide when the threatening email was first read and reported.

After the two different decisions became public and the threat was dismissed, Los Angeles officials stood by their decision "to be cautious," which can be perceived as both defensive and suggesting New York City was not. However, the decision to keep New York City schools open may have eliminated more risk than trying to close the schools.

But it begs the unanswered questions: what would New York City have done after 5:00 a.m. if the threat had been analyzed as credible? We will never know the answers to that question, which is one of the greatest challenges for reaching and committing to a decision by those charged with doing so.

It is the core of having crisis management plans and critical event response teams in place. It is the core of the book *Snow Day*.

CHAPTER 5

SHOOTING DOWN AMERICAN PASSENGER JETS

It is difficult to know if our nation's leaders ever faced a decision as difficult as authorizing the destruction of a passenger jet filled with civilians, as they did on 9/11. Garrett M. Graff's book *The Only Plane in the Sky: An Oral History of 9/11* provides a powerfully detailed account of the discussions and decisions that led to the order to shoot down flight 93 as it approached Washington, DC.

> Of the four hijacked planes that morning, three had already reached their targets. American Airlines flight 11 and United Airlines flight 175 had hit and destroyed the World Trade Center towers. American Airlines flight 77 had crashed into the Pentagon.

With President George Bush on Air Force One and Vice President Dick Cheney at the White House, the decision was made to shoot down any plane to stop more attacks. And Karl Rove, George Bush's senior advisor, is quoted in the book:

> *He said "Yes," then there was a pause as he listened. Then another "yes." You had an unreal sense of time that whole day. I don't know whether it was 10 seconds or two minutes. Then he said, "You have my authorization."*

Then he listened for a while longer. He closed off the conversation. He turned to us and said that he had just authorized the shoot-down of hijacked airliners.

While the order was given several times by Vice President Dick Cheney when repeatedly asked, it was not communicated to the pilots. Ultimately, the passengers on flight 93 overpowered the hijackers, sacrificing their lives and crashing the plane in Somerset County, Pennsylvania.

Cheney wrote in his autobiography,

At about 10:15, a uniformed military aide came into the room to tell me that a plane, believed hijacked, was eighty miles out and headed for D.C. He asked me whether our combat air patrol had authority to engage the aircraft. Did our fighter pilots have authority, in other words, to shoot down an American commercial airliner believed to have been hijacked? "Yes," I said without hesitation. A moment later he was back. "Mr. Vice President, it's sixty miles out. Do they have authorization to engage?" Again, yes.

At stake was the resiliency and continued functioning of the United States Government against the impact that the next attack would have. It was not known at the time, but the intended target was the US Capitol Building. However, with the plane heading toward Washington, DC, the White House was also a highly probable target.

The United States was highly prepared to defend against a military attack from outside its borders. But its defense system was not built to respond to threats within its own airspace. As the events of 9/11 unfolded, the gaps in information gathering and analysis, decision-making, communications, and response became horrifically evident.

Post-9/11, the US Government moved quickly. On September 14, 2001, Operation Nobel Eagle was launched as the military response focused on internal surveillance and control of sovereign airspace over Canada and the United States.

CHAPTER 6

CHOICES. DECISIONS. CONSEQUENCES

The following excerpt from the 9/11 Commission Report offers insight into the planning and resultant communications challenges that placed the United States in a reactive posture during the terrorist attacks. It also exemplifies the planning, redundancy, information and communications gaps that all enterprises face during a crisis or critical event.

Some of the major failures published in the report:

1. Lack of situational awareness. Most federal agencies learned of the first airliner hitting the World Trade Center on CNN.
2. Lack of accurate information. The President of the United States, George Bush, was at an elementary school visit in Florida and informed a small, twin engine plane had crashed into the World Trade Center, leading him and his staff to believe it was pilot error.
3. Lack of clear communication protocols: Teleconferences did not include the right officials from both the FAA and Defense Department. None succeeded in meaningfully coordinating the military and FAA. Numerous communication siloes and gaps resulted in significant communication gaps and lost response time.
4. A failure in decision authority and action: Vice President Cheney authorized fighter aircraft to engage the inbound plane (Flight 93) and shoot it down. That order never reached the pilots.
5. The military personnel expressed considerable confusion over the nature and effect of the order (to shoot down civilian airplanes) that did not respond.

The response on 9/11 included some business as usual behaviors. For example, Defense Secretary Donald Rumsfeld was having breakfast at the Pentagon with a group of members of Congress. He then returned to his office for his daily intelligence briefing. The Secretary's daily intelligence briefing took place in his Pentagon office, where he was informed of the second strike in New York and then resumed the briefing while awaiting more information.

This review of the 9/11 Commission Report's purpose is to set the stage for understanding and following crisis and critical event management strategies and planning. The adage, "plan your work, work your plan" fits well. Planning also identifies "What is at risk?" and "What might be lost?" thereby, answering the questions "What if we do?" and "What if we don't?"

The hard lessons learned from experiences, unanticipated business disruptions, critical events or catastrophic crises, like 9/11 and COVID-19, is that the money and time not invested in preparedness is lost at a high multiple in lives, dollars and recovery time.

The 9/11 Commission Report Chapter 1.3 National Crisis Management is in the Appendix to provide a full understanding of the lack of situational awareness and accurate information that blocked effective and timely decision making and decision authority communications.

II. THE LEADERSHIP INTERVIEWS

The following are narratives with SMEs (subject matter experts) on crisis and critical event management.

CHAPTER 7

MEET MAJOR GENERAL JACK BRIGGS

Major General Jack Briggs
US Air Force
(Retired)

The September 11 attacks put America's crisis management response plan into action. The most publicly recognized change was creating the Department of Homeland Security with its secretary a member of the Cabinet of the United States.

The United States military took more private crisis management actions. On September 14, 2001, Operation Nobel Eagle was launched as the military response to the 9/11 terrorist attacks. The Operation Nobel Eagle (ONE) mission is focused on internal surveillance and control of sovereign airspace over Canada and the United States. NORAD (North American Aerospace Defense Command) was already in place focusing on external airspace threats.

In 2002, NORTHCOM was created. The United States Northern Command "defends Our Homeland—Deters, detects, and defeats threats to the United States, conducts security cooperation activities with allies and partners, and supports civil authorities," per its website. NORAD and NORTHCOM were paired with a common, dual-hatted commander. There are two separate but complementary structures and staff in place—one for external and one for domestic airspace defense.

Jack Briggs was an Air Force major and F-117 pilot the day 9/11 happened. Ten years later, Jack's career intersected with the 9/11 terrorist attacks when he assumed the role of decision-maker in NORAD as a one-star general and deputy commander for the Canadian NORAD Region, including Operation Noble Eagle and NORTHCOM.

It was in that role and subsequent roles as vice commander of the Continental United States NORAD Region and ultimately director of operations for US Northern Command (2011–2017) that he was responsible for making the decisions to protect North America. In his new role, Jack faced many questions from leadership when a potential risk or event presented itself.

> The decision-making process was already in place when 9/11 happened. What changed was the institution of Operation Noble Eagle. I was charged with making recommendations about actions related to Event X, such as the terrorist attack on 9/11, a large wildfire or other crisis.

Jack is a serious and logical thinker who focuses on communicating about the decision-making process. As the commander of an organization of over three thousand people in Europe—responsible for administering all programs for operations, budgeting, welfare, and discipline, with an annual budget of $59 million and capital assets exceeding $1 billion—he was rated number one of six peer leaders in Europe, leading a senior commander to recognize, "JL makes every place better for the Air Force and Airmen."

> In my work, I learned to not get stuck thinking only about the most dangerous things that could happen. If I let myself think, "It could happen," my mind would run away to the absolute worst thing it could come up with. Most of those things, the most dangerous ones, turn out to be existential to the organization with little I could do to fix them. Instead, I spent more time addressing what was most likely to happen just short of existential. Those are the most likely large things, the really damaging events. In business resilience and disaster management planning, resilience against small things is typically well planned and responded to. Those are the most likely, small things

which organizations have operational flows and teams in place to handle the situation within their unit and recover.

But it is the most likely large things that significantly impact operations and overwhelm available resources. Having a crisis management plan and team in place with clear communications flows is critically important to the decision-making process and, as a result, the success of the organization's crisis management outcome. Once the process is in place to respond and solve for the most likely large event, the remediation action reduces it to a most likely small event.

Decisions related to an unlikely, but most dangerous event are decisions of survival. In business resilience, planning decisions are related to the most likely event with a large disruptive impact. These decisions are about how to keep things going. My initial focus is to ensure a process that gives us actionable information. The keys to success are to gather, synthesize and analyze data from which to make decisions. And you have to be assured that the data is trustworthy.

These data points can be from an internal organization, a contractor, or a media outlet such as the Weather Channel. But it should be a source from which you have been receiving a consistent presentation of synthesized and reliable information.

One hundred percent of the time, external facts have to be considered in the decision. For example, observing peer actions such as how similar organizations communicate and reach decisions as events progress speeds your own decision process. This is mostly related to large events that require big decisions about cost and time. Are you evacuating the facilities or closing operations for the day? The month, or maybe forever?

The next question to consider is: Who is the information going to?

Identifying the decision-maker early and ensuring they have the authority to make the final call is paramount to a successful response. That does not mean that person must come up with the options; instead, they must be ready to make choices among the options and the recommendation presented.

> Decision making is an inoculation to anxiety. One of the most valuable contributions the crisis management team leader can make to the ultimate decision-maker, is the incredible importance of deciding. Once that decision is made and communicated, the anxiety goes away. People have direction and are able to focus on execution.

> And knowing the person with authority is important to assure a working relationship is in place. Understanding their decision-making process, professional experience and personality improve communication even if the options communicated will be the same.

> You must follow a clear communications path based on the current situation. You must Stop The Imagination and focus on what is most likely to happen. Tell the decision-maker what you know, what you don't know, what you are doing about it, and who you recommend also needs to know. Only tell them things that are based on facts, no guessing. And explain those things that are important to know, but are not known due to external decision-making (such as awaiting a government authority to make a declaration) or events that have not happened yet (there may be a power outage and the A/B paths of that happening or not will determine recommendations).

Removing blind spots or potential disconnects that slow the decision-making process is also important. You need to overcommunicate. The team or person preparing options and a recommendation should explain exactly what they are doing and who they are in contact with—by name, title, and organization (such as a law enforcement or intelligence contractor resource).

And the question should be repeatedly asked: Who else needs to know? In a dynamic situation, pushing information up and out should be reevaluated and directed as appropriate.

And then you train and train and train, at every opportunity to be ready. A crisis will put you in a reactive place at first. But training to make initial decisions by using a checklist moves the people and the process quickly from reacting to doing something about it.

The checklist's initial use gives way to a calmer approach for solving the unique issues of the problem at hand by reviewing timing, personnel, resources, severity of the incident, and the risks. It moves the discussion to problem-solving.

And training gives you something to fall back on as you react to the problem. It gives you the momentum to take initial steps and then begin to think through the solution.

As an Air Force pilot, we trained over and over again with classwork, simulators, and even in the real aircraft, to be prepared for emergency situations. This could be an aircraft malfunction or combat. The key steps were burned into our brains if things didn't go as expected.

Step 1: Maintain Aircraft Control. This means focus on flying the airplane. It isn't likely to disintegrate around you. That is worst case and you can't do anything about that. That's why you have a parachute. You keep flying the plane and don't give up.

Step 2: Analyze the Situation. This means assessing what you know, and don't know and what you are going to do about it.

Step 3: Take Proper Action. This means knowing how the plane works and what steps to take to fix what you can, accept what you can't, and make decisions. The most dangerous thing is to not make any decisions at all. If you freeze debating what is the best answer, you will end up losing it all. Make the best decision with the information you have at the time, be adaptable as the situation changes, and push your mind to not over-react and try to start to think ahead to what is next. Think of it this way. A B– decision on time is better than an A+ decision late.

Step 4: Land as Soon as Conditions Permit. This means getting the aircraft on the ground as quickly and as safely as you can based on the conditions. If it is a training mission near your base, you can stop the training, head back to the base and land. If it is over enemy territory and you are hundreds of miles from home, you have to adapt to the situation with what you have, keep deciding, and never give up.

These four steps are specific to a plane you are flying but you can see the parallels to any crisis decision in business or life. Maintain control of the most important things that are core to your business. It may be keeping the information flowing or keeping your people safe. You won't control everything, but you will be focused on the important but not only the urgent. Urgency will eat up your bandwidth. Analyze the situation around you. Get the information you can and decide by taking proper action. Finally, land the issue causing the crisis as soon as the conditions permit. Be ready for a long fight if necessary, but never give up.

Training includes building relationships, understanding roles and expertise on the team. Agility is important to quickly identify options and make recommendations. In a crisis, time is critical to reduce its impact.

The expertise Jack crafted during his thirty-one-year service to the United States Air Force were put to work after his retirement in the private sector when he joined New York University as Vice President, Global Resiliency and Security.

Jack led NYU's "Emergency Management and Continuity, a Global Security Operations Center, a Communications Center, Fire Life Safety,

Global Academic Center Security Operations, and Security Technology for their 15 campuses in 11 countries protecting over 70,000 students, faculty, and administration" stakeholders. When COVID-19 arrived, he led the university's crisis management response: "I was a change agent instituting processes and procedures to build an agile and effective planning, mitigation, response, and recovery architecture to ensure readiness for the missions of teaching, research, and public service."

Jack used this process for organizing decision-making as a pilot, commander, and leader in the US Air Force, NORAD, NYU, and now as a CEO of a nonprofit. The roles changed, but the idea of leading through crisis has not, and having a plan before crisis strikes makes all the difference.

CHAPTER 8

THE PANDEMIC ARRIVES: 2019-nCoV OUTBREAK UPDATE @ ISMA

Dr. Myles Druckman
Group Medical Director for Health Innovation
International SOS
and
Stevan Bernard
Chief Executive Officer
Bernard Global, LLC

Among the professional associations supporting the top security executives at the largest companies in the world is the International Security Management Association (ISMA). To be considered for membership, your title must be chief security officer, and your company must have a minimum revenue of $2 billion. As timing would have it, ISMA holds their annual winter membership meeting each January. And in late January 2020, over two hundred members attended the San Diego meeting.

As fate would have it, Stevan Bernard was both a member of ISMA and on the planning committee for this event. Steve also serves as a senior security advisor to the International SOS group of companies, which helps businesses with health, security, and risk management solutions, including epidemics.

Through his work with International SOS, the pandemic's initial appearance in China and international spread was known to him. But it had not yet received broad media attention in the USA. With the meeting underway and the agenda preset, Steve felt that the yet unnamed COVID-19 virus was quickly becoming the elephant in the room. He mentioned this to other members of the committee, and they agreed. Steve suggested that Dr. Myles Druckman (a seasoned pandemic expert with International SOS) be asked to speak to the attendees. Steve called Dr. Druckman, who he had known for several years, and it was agreed that Dr. Druckman (Group Medical Director for Health Innovation) would present the next day.

Dr. Druckman is experienced, highly regarded, and frequently sought out, with an international list of corporate clients around the world. While returning from a trip to Australia in 2003, he noted the news on severe acute respiratory syndrome (SARS) while passing through the airports. By the time he reached his office, he had dozens of messages from company medical directors asking for advice to plan their response.

"The organizations that are most prepared are the ones that were hit hardest in a prior crisis. They do not spend on crisis management and business continuity out of the goodness of their hearts. You see some of the most sophisticated risk management and crisis planning at companies that learned from a prior event. There must be a rational reason for their behavior. For example, in high-risk industries where they have had and continue to have exposure, bad things happen to their people, their brand and their business. As a result, they insure themselves by preparing for disruption. These are the companies that will put safeguards in place and work to get ahead of a crisis," said Dr. Druckman.

As a result, Dr. Druckman, his clients, and the ISMA attendees have a common need to be at the pointy end of the stick.

"We are not only focusing on the horizon of what might become a big threat, but we are always preparing for how we will respond when incidents or disasters arrive. Having intelligence is vital. And we cannot always publicly share what we know due to political sensitivity. Having local resources on the ground and in the hospitals, verbally communicating what is happening leads to a better understanding of the situation and better decision-making," said Dr. Druckman.

Steve shared his experience, "This was a tremendous opportunity for our members to get in front of the pandemic and take a leadership position. Some attendees jumped all over the situation. Others shied away from it. But unless the company has a Chief Medical Officer, I feel this belongs squarely to the Chief Security Officer. The C-Suites and Boards look to their security leaders to step up during a business disruption like COVID-19."

For global companies, disruptions like COVID-19, SARS, Ebola hit different places at different times unevenly, disrupting supply chains, work sites, and human resources. Adjusting to these unique situations requires interpreting data to fit the company's business and situation.

Part of the International SOS and Dr. Druckman's work included creating a software solution that digitized response plans. The Enterprise Health Security Center solution has a long history migrating from a paper to a digital product.

"International SOS has been providing corporate pandemic plans for over 20 years. The plans were traditionally in paper binders. Companies were looking for planning tools that were not only on-line but would be updated when required. It was clear that these global health threats evolve and recommendations and guidance changes frequently, but companies did not have the resources to maintain the content. International SOS, in partnership with several tech and finance companies developed the 'Enterprise Health Security Center' which is a web based, customizable tool that stores the latest tools and resources to manage not only pandemics but other threats like a Measles or Dengue Fever outbreak, a hurricane, wildfire or a terrorist attack," explained Dr. Druckman.

The system has best practice checklists, templates, communications, and tools to help an organization plan and respond to global threats. The program began in 2016 and was critical in supporting the Zika crisis and measles global outbreaks, as well as recent fires and hurricanes. When the coronavirus evolved in China, the platform created within days a "New Respiratory Illness" plan even before the disease had a name. Since then, the platform has over 150 documents and tools added and is maintained 24-7 to support COVID-19 preparation, return-to-work and return-to-travel actions. It is used by over seven hundred organizations. The COVID-19 content continues to be updated and is used by organizations to orient their personnel and help ensure business is maintained.

Dr. Druckman's first awareness of COVID-19 was in December 2019, before the wet market in Wuhan was closed on New Year's Day 2020 when disturbing stories about people becoming ill arose. "The first analysis was that it spread from animal to person, but not person to person. We monitored the situation and heard concerning news that people were becoming ill who were not at the market," said Dr. Druckman.

As the head of International SOS's China practice for four years earlier in his career, he experienced the government's lack of transparency during SARS and believes, as a result, they were more forthcoming with information when COVID-19 struck.

"There are a number of underground resources that physicians communicate through to get information, such as Promed. Many of the communications from China pointed to the magnitude of the virus being significant.

"During the time I presented to the ISMA Conference, I was also meeting one on one with our clients to help them prepare their COVID-19 plan," shared Dr. Druckman. He was especially focused on building their internal mechanisms to decide when to pull the trigger on their response programs. And to ensure the resources were in in place and ready to support the volume of work needed to respond effectively.

As a result, he advised clients to be overly nervous and aggressive in their response and scale it back, if appropriate. But the analysis was right on target as most businesses and governments were not aggressive enough and health care systems were overwhelmed.

Among the factors considered is the resilience of the health care system in a specific area. Some countries have strong public health care resources in place while others do not. That resilience level impacts how clients are advised to manage a health-related situation.

"We could give options and recommendations based on our analysis to ten clients and have ten different levels of response depending on the business they are in, where they do business and their risk tolerance," said Dr. Druckman.

At the time COVID-19 was spreading, many companies had been preparing for an influenza pandemic, H1N1, which luckily was milder than anticipated. There was still concern for a big pandemic flu, which is transmitted as a respiratory illness like COVID-19. Fortunately, companies that investigated the pandemic flu and updated their response preparations made the risk management decision to purchase significantly more PPE than usual. Their crisis management planning for the flu strengthened their response to the coronavirus.

The title slide named the pandemic "2019-nCoV Outbreak Update," and his presentation was prescient.

2019-nCoV Outbreak Update

ISMA January 2019

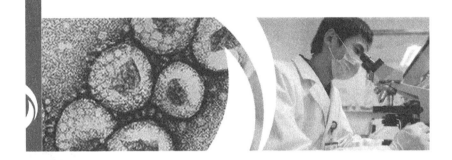

Stating that there was much to learn, the disease would be particularly dangerous for those who were older or had preexisting conditions. And that it would be contagious before the infected person showed any symptoms.

The Disease
Much still to Learn

Potential High Risk Groups:

- Underlying medical conditions (diabetes, Hypertension, Cardiovascular Disease, etc)
- Older age

- Contagious before symptoms?
- Incubation 3-10 days?

WORLDWIDE REACH. HUMAN TOUCH.

2

35

Dr. Druckman then helped managers by outlining an immediate action plan:

- Focus on employees who travel, have international assignments, and are local staff in affected areas.
- Communications have to be succinct and immediate to prevent illness and contain spread.
- Employees should be screened at points of entry and wear PPE.
- All facilities need to be thoroughly cleaned and sanitized to reduce spread.
- Where possible, employees should move to remote work environments.

What Security Managers Should Consider

Create a new plan for:

- Travelers
- International Assignees
- Local Staff

- In "affected areas"
- Outside "affected areas"

- Communication
- Point-of-entry Screening
- Personal Protective Equipment
- Cleaning
- Remote work / Virtual meetings
- Monitor and modify the plan

- Long distance Run

WORLDWIDE REACH. HUMAN TOUCH.

Dr. Druckman included the following points demonstrating what was and not known at the time:

- Shocking but important: this virus is new
- Human-to-human spread (efficient?)
- Much unknown, much more to learn
- China focus today—tomorrow?

Summary

- A new coronavirus
- Capable of causing severe infection
- Symptoms – fever, shortness of breath
- Human to human spread (efficient?)
- Much unknown, much more to learn
- Create a plan and ACTIVATE
- China focus today – tomorrow?
- Keep Monitoring

WORLDWIDE REACH. HUMAN TOUCH.

4

37

Encouraging all attendees to activate their crisis management plans, he presented a stark and unsettling accurate future on his final slide:

- Continuous spread
- "Clusters" of outbreaks in certain communities
- Major disruption in "affected" areas—Wuhan almost shut down
- Supply chain issues
- Fear to go *outside*—impact on *customer*
- Outbreaks at different times at different places—"waves"
- Treatment—unlikely for a while
- Vaccine—unlikely for longer

No workplace is the *same*

Future

- Continuous Spread to other countries
- "Clusters" of outbreaks in certain communities
- Major disruption in "affected" areas – Wuhan almost shut down
- Supply chain issues
- Fear to go "Outside" – impact "customer"
- Outbreaks at different times at different places – "Waves"
- Treatment – unlikely for awhile
- Vaccine – unlikely for longer
- No workplace is the SAME

WORLDWIDE REACH. HUMAN TOUCH.

Dr. Druckman noted, "We have been and still are working with 1000s of clients on their programs." For example, they are helping clients set up the infrastructure for vaccinations worldwide, including communicating the process and tracking progress.

Steve stated, "For some in security this may have been a missed opportunity that may not be recoverable. Not everyone 'stepped up' to this challenge, for a variety of reasons. Some of the CSO's who acted after the ISMA meeting have greater responsibilities today. Some may not have survived the aftermath."

Steve Bernard continues to have a storied and influential career not just in risk management and security, but in business management as a thought leader. Like many, he started in law enforcement and moved to private security and earned his way to being executive vice president at Sony Pictures. He is no stranger to crises, including the "Fukushima Daiichi earthquake-caused" nuclear disaster in 2011 and the Guardians of Peace cyberattack in 2014.

Steve explained, "The 2011 Level 9 earthquake > tsunami (referred to as the Fukushima Daiichi nuclear disaster) had unimaginable, extensive 'ripple' effects. Contamination affected people, land, air and water. The nearby town of 150,000 was evacuated. 500,000 people were left homeless. Every Pacific rim country was in some way affected. It was not possible to quickly assess impacts or the severity/risk of aftershocks. However, because of the prevalence of earthquakes certain systems are pre-programmed to shut down to then allow risk assessments. The Tokyo rail systems being one. This is the primary mode of transit for worker's in this city of nearly 10 million citizens. Tokyo is home to Sony's HQ. At the time, I worked at Sony Pictures Entertainment in Los Angeles. Sony employed roughly 65,000 personnel in Japan. A few weeks following this incident I was in Tokyo and I met with various leaders from Sony. I never forgot those conversations. Imagine the following: it is about 3PM on Friday and you are responsible for either a department, division, factory, or office complex. Or perhaps you are the CEO. Employees are rightfully fearful and confused, media stories are conflicting, communications are down, transit of all modes is down, power is only sporadic, and the ground is still shaking.

"The distance between Fukushima and Tokyo is only 238 kilometers. What do you tell your staff? Stay put or go home? It's a decision each individual must make based upon the best possible information available. If you decide to stay do you know how stable the facility is? What resources are available (sustenance, power, water, etc.)? How will you be able to determine the status of loved ones? What if you decide to go home? For some who did, the walk took half a day or more. The assumption that basic resources (food and water) would be available along the journey was a bad one. Key supplies dwindled very fast. Many brave people did many brave things that day and for many months following. My point here, contingency planning should always consider worse case scenarios however hard to imagine they may be."

Recent polls by Pew Research and Edelman show that employees expect their employers to have crisis management programs in place. Overall, they trust their organizations more than the local authorities for advice.

Steve said, "This is evolving. As government revenues continue to decline, so will the economy and the services we have received from them. Employees reliance on and trust in their employers for crisis management will grow."

Dr. Druckman agrees, "It is important for the employers to share a strategy and communicate because their employees will depend on them first. Should they go to work? When? What about their family, income, work tasks? These are the first critical questions an employer has to be ready to address. The benefit is the trust employees will proffer to you."

The government authorities and businesses have different stakeholders and dynamics, leading to different decision flows. The government is focused on public health and containing the virus. Businesses are focused on resilience and continuity. Masks are a good example. For businesses, getting PPE to their employees to stay open and be safe was number one on their list. And for many, they had stockpiled PPE to prepare for the flu and were ready. But public health authorities did not initially recommend wearing masks because they did not have enough supply to distribute.

Steve's experience offers great insight to the real-world work of crisis management planning: "Being informed is important. Continually gathering and analyzing data is part of security's function. And that enables preparedness. You cannot prepare for everything, but you can prepare a framework to customize from. You also have to have permission to be wrong. Lastly, you have to confirm who has the authority to decide. Not knowing is the biggest inhibitor to making good decisions."

CHAPTER 9

MISSION IMPOSSIBLE FOODS

George McCloskey
Vice President, Safety and Security
Impossible Foods

"I brought the pandemic to my organization," shares George McCloskey of Impossible Foods. And *impossible* is a good adjective for his start at the company. He joined Impossible Foods on January 6, 2020, as its first safety and security leader, charged with creating and executing a risk management, safety and security program. In a positive twist of fate, George was the chair for the late January 2020 ISMA meeting in San Diego (detailed in chapter 8).

After seeing reports of the virus abroad, and hearing a discussion on the topic through various intelligence organizations, Stevan Bernard suggested that we have Dr. Miles Druckman address the topic at our Conference.

At the time, there were only 887 reported cases in mainland China and no known deaths.

Dr. Druckman's presentation and George's experience led to two conclusions that the threat was highly credible and could be highly disruptive to his company's business.

On 1/29/2020 I emailed our General Counsel and senior executives after attending the Conference and suggested that we start planning for workplace impacts, and that we should halt all "non-essential" business travel to China. I also suggested a company-wide email message that in retrospect, contained all the current information regarding a healthy workplace that we are seeing today. I sent that message to the entire company on 1/29/2020.

It was bold action for a new leader in the C-suite who would not even have a budget approved until six months later. But he was hired for this exact moment that just happened to arrive during his first days on board.

It was also my introduction to everyone at the company as I had just started in my role on 1/6/2020. But being new and not having a mature risk management program in place at Impossible Foods was both a liability and a blessing. Creating a structured program takes many years in the making including team building, defining roles and responsibilities and training.

However, business resilience is often a discussed versus an acted-upon discipline: "No company I have ever worked at puts serious time and investment to build that muscle. Business resilience tends to be extra work on top of the day job. Many organizations do not put significant resources into this skill set and therefore have longer cycles to get good at it.

"At the same time, we did not have the traditional, what I call 'security theater' that might get in the way of quick decision-making. What our industry calls guns, guards and gates. So, our organization was very fast to respond, and really developed momentum in planning right away. And again, because my company did not have a security or crisis management organization with any developed plan. Many eyes were on me to lead our response as the Vice President of Safety and Security. I had no staff, no budget, and no contracted resources to help. We developed a COVID-19 Team that consisted of our CEO Staff and his direct reports to meet and develop a mitigation response for the company. We met daily for about 6 weeks, and went to weekly meetings after we had employee, production, and office safety measures in place. We were blessed with leadership at the company that consisted of scientists and elite business leaders that were decisive, crisp, and unfailingly focused."

Impossible Foods is designated as an essential business, and deciding what functions and employees were essential and needed to be in the company facility was a core analysis that directed their decision tree. They focused on R&D and Production as the only essential departments. All other employees would work remotely, putting pressure on IT to facilitate remote online work support and information security. And HR and Legal to define and formalize the policy. For example, did it mean an employee could work from anywhere in the world, forever?

Alongside the safety response, Impossible Foods was forced to undergo a dramatic business response too. The company primarily sold to restaurants, which were closing and canceling their orders. They pivoted to selling to and through food stores, successfully.

George's acquired expertise helped him manage in this crisis. While there was no formal training in place for a pandemic, they put mandatory protocols, including weekly testing of every employee who is essential and entering the workplace.

> So, we shut down the workplace to all employees until we could put some basics in place. We only allowed "essential" staff to return to the facilities. Because we were classified as an "essential business" as a food manufacturer, we had to internally classify what positions were essential. Office staff was not essential; however, Production and R&D staff were. We immediately deployed a question set on our guest management system, and had every employee who needed to be physically at work go through the workflow prior to entry. We also started testing every person coming into the office and factory on a weekly basis.

> The COVID-19 Team also shut out the distractions that might slow or result in incorrect analysis and decisions. The team was chaired by our Chief of Staff whose leadership kept us on point and focused.

> All of the security industry "ambulance chasers" came out of the woodwork initially, with some solutions that

bordered on ridiculous. We did not jump at them, but relied on a calm approach with proven technologies that worked and were practical. We avoided temperature scanning and always followed CDC guidelines as they developed. And we relied on the local county health departments to get factual information and ensure compliance.

Because a risk management program was not in place, Impossible Foods had no built-in capabilities. George reflects, "We did not have an Emergency Notification System (ENS) and will be developing one this year. That would have helped especially for contact tracing. We also do not have an internal Wiki or bulletin board system, which would have helped in disseminating information to employees." The company relied on email and Slack but realized they also needed an ENS (emergency notification system) and disaster response structure.

Underlying the pandemic response are the basic blocking and tackling of managing a budget and demonstrating value to the company's stakeholders. But COVID-19 forced dramatic organizational changes to how companies operate and how and where their employees, supply chains, and customers work.

To work around the issues of budget planning and approval during the pandemic's onset, the company created a COVID project budget where all related expenses were entered, such as facility changes and testing. "This allowed us to execute quickly, where the default answer was assumed to be 'yes' when unplanned spending was needed."

Organizationally, the company realized in 2019 it needed a dedicated safety and security function and hired George to lead the organization. But George's organization chart has not changed. Had the positions been in place, directors of global security, business continuity and resilience, and environmental health and safety would have provided additional expertise and support to the company's response.

But my role was changed and will change back this year. I will shift my focus from being 90% tactical, to 90% strategic this year—that is what I expected would happen in 2020 except for the pandemic!

Moving forward in 2021 we will develop a DR response, hold tabletops in order to develop the muscle needed to navigate any business disruption. This will not happen overnight, and organizations need to know this. It takes time, effort, and a commitment to business resilience. It takes an understanding and devotion to Duty of Care for your employees as well, something more and more companies are loath to embrace.

As these functions are built out inside of the company, George will also focus outside the company on its supply chain: "We need to focus intently on our BCP plan, as well as third-party risk. Do our business partners have a BCP plan? Are their DR systems exercised? How do we incorporate our expectations of those with whom we partner into our legal contracts? How do we audit those readiness plans? Is our IT infrastructure adequate?" Great risk management thinkers will tirelessly peel the onion layer by layer, finding more vulnerabilities and working to understand them, and recommend ways to their internal business customer to reduce or eliminate them. In the end, it is the business that decides what risks and related disruptions they will spend money to mitigate.

Reflecting on the past year, George recognized his background helped prepare him to manage in a crisis. "Those that work in law enforcement, fire and EMS response have tremendous practice and training because they have always only been needed in emergencies," he pointed out.

But having practice making decisions during an emergency with clarity and calmness comes with time.

Crises happen all the time. I have not been with an organization that has not been through a crisis.

Information security is a good example of a function that is always responding to attacks and potential crises. They have become very good at managing events. That muscle memory makes you a good crisis manager in general. But COVID-19 was new and hard to get information on. That made fact-based response planning more difficult.

Companies faced conflicting information and opinions as the virus was politicized. By making sound recommendations, in this case, relying on CDC (Centers for Disease Control) and county health departments, as well as a group of internal science officers, George brought focus and calm to the response, solidifying George's position as the go-to leader.

> What worked for us were science-based approaches that were practical. We followed the CDC guidelines, not the hype. We also tested every employee and contractor that was coming into the workplace, and we did this weekly at great expense. Testing was perhaps the game changer, accompanied by regular messaging and discussions held company wide. We have a weekly "all-hands" meeting where we communicate what we are doing and why. We really had to work hard to help people understand that it was safe for them to come into our facilities.

Asked if his company is ready to call a snow day, he shared that there is work to be completed at this newly-stood-up organization, including developing a crisis management organization that can monitor world events and respond appropriately in the year ahead.

> The Covid-19 pandemic of 2020 helped to invigorate the need for security programming that is focused on duty of care issues for our organizations. Post 9/11, we have forgotten about the importance of having a well-developed response plan to address business interruptions. Security leaders should continue to work within their organizations to develop the internal relationships that can help advocate for the resources needed to support their work. Business resilience, or the lack of it, is an existential threat to the survival of the company. We have been focused on physical security risks (intrusion, active shooter, insider, etc.) that are important, and have different recovery drivers. I am not dismissing these types of events as they have widespread and lasting impacts if not mitigated. But as leaders we need to build our programming to include risks against revenue, operations, and employee well-being.

CHAPTER 10

BEYOND RESILIENCE

Joe Olivarez
Vice President
Jacobs

At the core of Jacobs' crisis management program is their dedicated focus on operational excellence and their innovative BeyondZero program. Their BeyondZero program has a straightforward mission statement:

> Work must be healthy, safe and secure for our people and our planet. We go beyond our workplace and into our daily lives, creating a safer and healthier future for our families and our communities.

> BeyondZero is the foundation of our company's culture of caring and a core part of our values and who we are at Jacobs. We are proud that in our culture, our people go beyond following rules, procedures and processes. Our goal is beyond driving statistics to zero. Although we have made significant progress since we commenced our BeyondZero journey in 2007, our performance can always be better. It is imperative that through our common vision and purpose, we continue to improve together, Challenging Today Reinventing Tomorrow.

The goal is to ambitiously and in a sustainable manner continuously improve in our HSE (Health, Safety & Environmental) and security performance, lift the wellbeing of our employees and our partners, and increase our business resilience. We tackle all types of harm at work. This includes continuing our focus on acute harm associated with high-risk activities, while ensuring we are managing wider health risks, including mental health and working from home. (www.jacobs.com)

Jacobs' is also laser focused on operational excellence as a core part of its culture and business strategy. Its Center for Operational Excellence augments the Line of Business capability to support acceleration of the company's performance. Jacobs is a major consultancy for customers that "has played a major role in many of the most complex deployments of EHS information management solutions in the world under arduous performance, cost, and schedule metrics."

Joe Olivarez is the vice president of the Operations Center for Excellence and the company's chief security officer. It is this focus that enabled the company to have one global crisis management program in place for any event, including COVID-19.

Joe explains, "The structure for crisis management was strongly in place when the pandemic arrived. We had one plan systematically deployed globally integrating emergency management to crisis management. It was up and running on Day 1. Jacobs' COO, Bob Pragada, is the crisis leader with coordination from the Global Security & Resilience Office."

Jacobs is committed to the protection and sustainability of people, the environment and assets for all stakeholders, both internal and external, as well as Jacobs personnel; this includes clients, partners, contractors, and local communities. To achieve this, Jacobs Global Security & Resilience (GS&R) adopts an integrated approach to risk management that both anticipates threat and develops resilience through proportionate application of mitigation measures that seek to both create and protect value throughout a project life cycle.

To support this, Jacobs GS&R provides a multiskilled team with significant experience that enables real insight in relation to the various challenges of global operations. Critical within this approach is the organization's ability to respond to an emergency or crisis while maintaining business continuity.

The structure includes three regional crisis management teams in Asia, the Americas, and EMEA that lead our operational execution and report to the global crisis management team. The executive vice presidents and representatives from Legal, HR, IT, Real Estate, Communications, Operations, Finance Security, and HSE from each region are on the respective crisis teams. The three region crisis management teams are supported by country crisis teams and/or emergency management team hubs.

"We responded immediately. First, was concern for our employees. We wanted to let them know we were working on the situation and thinking about them and their well-being first. Next, we wanted to communicate our resilience to our clients and assure their confidence in us to execute on some of the most challenging projects in the world. Next, we focused on execution. We identified about 20% of our global workforce that would be required to work at a company or customer location. That allowed 80% of our workforce to work remotely," said Joe.

Jacobs worked both internally and externally to ensure that the best safety practices including self-health monitoring, temperature checks, PPE proper ergonomics, and social distancing were being followed within Jacobs facilities, at client locations, and at home.

Joe shared the internal questions and thinking: "As the pandemic has evolved to living and working in a COVID world—the vaccine and how it will contribute to the overall operating environment improvement is top of mind for our employees. Will it help us return to the office faster, I am an expat deployed in a locale where I am not comfortable with the options— what are my options, I am client critical and I need to travel—what can I do or not do, etc.? The company is now focused on communicating about and supporting vaccinations for their employees."

They informed all their stakeholders that they were researching the vaccine issue and formulating policy on whether all employees would be required to be vaccinated before they returned to work. They also communicated that the current safety programs being used were working effectively.

Second, they focused on employees who would be required to be vaccinated before returning to a worksite, typically per a client requirement. Members of the crisis management team coordinated with Legal to build out the legal framework for vaccination policy. For example, some Jacobs employees work at government agencies that would be getting the vaccines directly, and their employees would be vaccinated through those agencies. But not every employee may want to be vaccinated. Or may not be comfortable going back to work. The company worked through this process quickly and empathetically.

Finally, the global company had to craft one core communication related to vaccinations. Do they mandate them? Do they highly encourage them? Communicating a core position that worked globally was important; however, it needed to be adaptable for the regional crisis teams to adjust as appropriate for local country requirements and situational context.

"As a company, we have focused our time on value, process, efficiency, execution and accountability that contributes to the real messaging around resiliency. That investment is what led to having the crisis management framework in place for an effective response," said Joe. In fact, Jacobs' adjustments to personnel operational levels have been small during the pandemic, demonstrating the company's resiliency during the crisis.

At the hub of the crisis management operation was information collection, synthesis, and distribution; as Joe explained, "We have the process to gather and centralize the information where we put eyes on it and produce an output. We created a Return-to-Work sub team that supported the Global Crisis Management Team. The group researched and assessed best practices, benchmarks, what peer companies were doing and how customers were responding to inform our leaders. This same group developed enhanced processes such as Real Estate and HSE&S readiness inspections. We developed a decision guidance tool that mapped all our operating locations and incorporated local information related to 3-, 7-, and 14-day case rate trend, national restriction levels, ICU bed capacity, case rate per/100K, etc. This allowed us to look at the situation globally and helped determine what offices/operations were in a more permissive environment that would afford us the opportunity to open and execute safely and efficiently. This capability allowed to us to better educate leadership by being better informed and creating the bandwidth for them to focus on decision making and operation execution. A focus their business. When the recommended Return to Work program was presented, they understood it and were aligned with its goals to safely reopen and stay open."

The crisis management teams distributed similar information on vaccine progress. "The technology and the tracking reporting can get skewed. We provide a weekly report summarizing global vaccine information to create an understanding of what is happening in the world and the reasons for the recommendations being made," said Joe.

The information sources analyzed were many, and each added value to the data-driven decisions reached by the Jacobs crisis management team, including these helpful resources:

1. IHS Markit's risk intelligence business is a specialist intelligence provider that forecasts commercially relevant economic, political, and violent risks worldwide. The risk portal within their offering delivers geospatial risk intelligence and reliable forecasts to multiple sectors, including insurance/reinsurance, financial services, corporate, banking, governments, nongovernment organizations (NGOs), shipping, oil and gas, aviation, mining, cargo, logistics, and media. The company offers valuable online briefing sessions.

"They track verticals, such as the pharmaceutical industry, which is a significant customer base for Jacobs, and inform on what supply chain security needs they will face in the future. This is extremely helpful," noted Joe.

2. Gartner, primarily known for IT research, has been informative on vaccine issues and how companies should think about them, including the following:

    •   Management of remote employees
    •   Vaccine rollout management
    •   Distribution questions for supply chain leaders
    •   Requirement of employees to be vaccinated
    •   Questions before resetting post-pandemic business strategy

3. The Society for Human Resource Management (SHRM) has been a useful resource on social responsibility, human rights, and sustainability.

"If you have the desire, like I have, to be a perfectionist and dig through these issues, then SHRM's information is very helpful," commented Joe.

Jacobs is a customer of both International SOS and World Aware. Both were valuable sources for COVID-19 intelligence and strategic thinking during the pandemic.

"Everbridge has played a central role in the company's GSOC supporting its global security programs. The company is playing a pivotal role for mass notification of our personnel across the globe. As countries, states and local municipalities were issuing and/or amending restriction and/or travel notices this allowed us to timely and effectively communicate with our employees.

"They are very quick and agile," Joe said.

The demand for information and intelligence is never waning. "Boards of Directors are asking more and more questions, and that is good. They are always asking about cyber security. Sustainability questions have been increasing in recent years. And I see Enterprise Risk Management (ERM) on the rise as a result of the COVID-19 pandemic. At Jacobs we have an Enterprise Risk Management Office and we continue to collaborate to manage the operational challenges and opportunities that may come our way," said Joe.

"The Board of Directors and the Executive Leadership Team have a significant fiduciary responsibility and they continue to ask the critical questions necessary to protect the interests of our corporations. It is imperative that the function chartered with developing, educating and executing the crisis management program is constantly planning and preparing. In addition, it must help shape and foster an environment that is transparent leading to meaningful discussions and resulting is positive outcomes.

"If this environment is present, success is within reach," concluded Joe.

Reflecting on the past year and the challenges ahead, Joe shared, "During the pandemic we divested a $3 billion dollar piece of business and executed several acquisitions successfully while at the same time executing our crisis plan in response to COVID-19. Having a flexible and well-positioned framework enabled the company to meet the challenges and be resilient.

"The Global Security & Resilience has many years of crisis management leadership experience—myriad of issues (weather, terrorism, industrial accidents, etc.) In addition, the emergency and crisis management program has been up and running for years managing terrorism events, natural disasters, etc. that have impacted their operations directly or indirectly. The company also trains and exercises teams on an annual basis. Having dedicated communications and disaster recovery plans in place that are integrated into their global crisis management plan ensured the company was well prepared to manage the unforeseen pandemic crisis.

"The goal is to protect the business. And we did."

CHAPTER 11

WORLD CHAMPIONSHIP RESILIENCE!

Jeff Miller
Vice President and Chief Security Officer
The Kansas City Chiefs

The Kansas City Chiefs had just defeated the San Francisco 49ers in Super Bowl LIV on February 2, 2020. But shortly after Super Bowl LIV, professional and amateur sports, live concerts, theater, trade shows, and conventions around the world were being postponed or canceled to reduce COVID-19's spread. On March 11, 2020, the World Health Organization declared COVID-19 a pandemic. On March 12, the National Basketball Association suspended its season.

It was now the off-season for professional football, and the players were on a well-earned break and not required back at work until July 28, and their first full-contact practice would not happen until August 17. At the time, there was optimism "normal" would return by early summer and that the NFL's upcoming season would not be interrupted.

In Kansas City, the early odds favored the NFL's Super Bowl champion Kansas City Chiefs to repeat as champions in Super Bowl LV on February 7, 2021. And the NFL's thirty-one other teams would be preparing to claim the championship as their own come July.

In early March of 2020, Jeffrey Miller and the Chiefs' management team were back at work holding planning discussions as the pandemic became more prevalent overseas. And they took immediate action, coordinated with the National Football League to address the pandemic's risk.

> Our organization has a dynamic executive leadership team that collaborates with our Team President and Ownership group to chart the course of the organization in responding to threats to the business. Enterprise Risk Management is ingrained within our business planning process on an annual basis.
>
> While we did not have a specific pandemic plan, we immediately developed a communications plan and limited access to our facilities to only essential personnel. We developed entry protocols to include temperature screening and a medical questionnaire and developed a custom app for employees to use. We immediately developed an Infectious Disease Emergency Response plan for both our practice facility and our stadium that was approved by the NFL Chief Medical Officer.

That is Dr. Allen Sills, who became the NFL's first full-time CMO, "dedicated to advancing the health and safety of the sport of football," in March 2017. Dr. Sills joined the league from Vanderbilt University Medical Center, where he continued to serve at Vanderbilt as a professor of neurological surgery and the founder and codirector of the Vanderbilt Sports Concussion Center.

His initial work focused on the health and safety of the players to reduce injuries. Working with team medical staff and committee members built working relationships and a communications cadence that would enable robust discussion and decision-making related to COVID-19 response.

Dr. Sills has led the NFL's response to the COVID-19 pandemic, in consultation with the NFL and NFLPA medical advisors, including the infectious disease experts at Infection Control for Sports (ICS) and epidemiologists from IQVIA, in addition to guidance from the Centers for Disease Control and Prevention (CDC) and other public health officials.

The team leveraged the expert advice and support from the NFL as well as put its own crisis management plans into action.

Jeff shared, "The pandemic heightened the safety aspect of my role, but I have always been closely involved in enterprise risk management. Our executive leadership group and organization wide communication protocols that were in place supported our pandemic response. We functioned effectively, although differently, in the virtual environment."

For example, the organization moved to virtual training programs, but provided all of the planned training to their internal and external partners. They formed new working groups and named an infection control officer for the practice facility and the stadium.

> Probably the biggest takeaway is that we can do a large percentage of our jobs remotely with the use of technology. The pandemic operating environment does require additional communication efforts to keep everyone in the loop and helps to reduce any feelings of isolation on the part of some employees. One advantage of working from home has been a much better work/life balance for employees used to spending many hours every week away from their families.

The team also focused on leveraging existing technology to reduce spreading infections inside their facilities. "The Envoy access control and visitor management system was very helpful. Also, our extensive HD camera network was essential in controlling access remotely." They also added touchless temperature screening that tied in to the visitor management system, thereby locking out access for anyone registering an above-normal-range temperature.

The inside of their facilities were changed to ensure a safe and healthy environment, including modifications to the locker rooms, weight training areas, and meeting rooms. They also expanded command post locations to increase awareness and communications across the organization.

> Like any business managing through a crisis, and in this case a health related one, there were many actions taken to ensure resilience that included the safety of all stakeholders. None of these were budgeted expenditures, of course, but our President, Mark Donovan and Chairman and CEO, Clark Hunt relied on the crisis management team's recommendations as well as NFL guidance, and we were able to implement the changes allowing for continued operations.

As the summer approached, the NFL and all team members, including the Chiefs, kept vigilant on the battle against the pandemic and the successes and setbacks other leagues and events were facing. As the season approached, a major health and business decision needed to be made: Would there be fans at the games? Ultimately this would be decided by the individual teams. Across the league, some teams did not allow fans at the games while others did.

The Kansas City Chiefs worked with Dr. Rex Archer, the city's health director, who was skeptical that having fans at the games would work. As he told the *Kansas City Star* before the season began, "Is it a 100% foolproof from the disease spreading? No. Do we think we've taken a lot of precautions? Yes. Should folks that are high risk for hospitalization or death be attending? Probably not."

And the stadium greatly reduced its capacity to 22 percent or about 16,700 of the 76,000 seats being filled. As the season concluded, Dr. Archer expressed his pleasure with the experience and results as an unqualified success, as he told Michael Ryan of the *Kansas City Star* on January 10, 2021:

> *"There's actually no question that it's been successful,"* *Archer told me. "We've not actually had any cases traced to exposure at the games. I'm particularly pleased with how this has gone."*

> *In fact, advance testing of those headed to Arrowhead Stadium's indoor suites prevented an average of four to a dozen or more COVID-positive fans from even attending.*

> *Indeed, the team's extensive planning and collaboration with Archer last summer became something of a model for the National Football League.*

> *"It kind of became the standard for those NFL stadiums that were going to be able to allow fans at all. They kind of looked at our approach. I had some meetings with NFL leadership," he says.*

> *Archer initially recommended against attending games,*

which The Star Editorial Board did as well and still stands by. Yet, Archer does suspect there's one surprising and happy byproduct of allowing fans in: They might otherwise have watched the games in a bar, restaurant or home-based gathering—indoor venues much more conducive to virus spread.

So, in short, that may have served to reduce community spread, he says.

Archer credits the entire Chiefs organization for its cooperation and responsiveness to his every safety suggestion.

"There's never been any pushback. You have a good, quality organization and it makes life a lot easier," Archer says. "The reason the Chiefs win isn't just because of their great players and coaches. But they have a solid organization at every level."

And the Chiefs did an outstanding job of overcommunicating with fans through local media, their website, and social media on best practices, including how to prepare before the game, plan for the game, and even protocols for leaving the stadium. As Michael Ryan reported,

The Chiefs' success—and Archer's, to be honest—is, unsurprisingly, the result of masks, carefully calibrated distancing (even in parking lots) and orderly and controlled pursuit of concessions and restrooms. In addition, after the preseason pep rally events and the first few games had revealed lagging mask usage after eating and drinking and as the hours wore on, the Chiefs responded with more late-game PA system reminders— and even pre-printed "wear your mask" signs for ushers to flash at patrons from a distance.

The NFL's work was also critical to the successful season. In the week leading up to Super Bowl LV, the *Wall Street Journal* reported that a CDC study from October 2020 was a wake-up call for the NFL:

It was early October, and the <u>NFL</u> had a problem. It wasn't just that players and staff for <u>the Tennessee Titans</u> were continuing to test positive in an outbreak that shook the NFL's season. It wasn't even that the league was learning that the virus was able to rush through holes in its protocols.

The NFL was slowly discovering something far deeper: a core tenet of COVID-19 transmission wisdom—how to define when individuals are in "close contact"—was just wrong.

The safety of interactions during <u>this global pandemic</u> had been for months measured by a stopwatch and a tape measure. The guidance was that someone had been exposed to the virus if they had been within six feet of an infected person for more than 15 minutes. It was drilled into everyone for so long it became <u>coronavirus gospel</u>.

But that wasn't proving true <u>during the NFL's outbreaks</u>. People were testing positive for the virus even though they had spent far less than 15 minutes or weren't within six feet of an infectious person—and the league had the contact-tracing technology to prove it.

"That was a wake-up call," said Dr. Allen Sills, the NFL's chief medical officer. "We had to be more precise in our definition of high-risk close contacts because clearly transmission could occur outside those basic boundaries of time and distance."

The league's finding is the critical reason why the NFL got through its regular season playing all 256 games and made it all the way to the upcoming <u>Super Bowl</u> on Sunday, between the <u>Tampa Bay Buccaneers</u> and <u>Kansas City Chiefs</u>, as scheduled.

The league's work and communications to enhance their safety protocols reduced the spread and contributed greatly to a successful and complete schedule.

The Kansas City Chiefs' positive experience managing the crisis led their team leadership to another decision. They agreed to be a polling location for the November 2020 election. Arrowhead Stadium is a perfect venue, being large, open, and having plenty of parking. With social distancing built in, the team again stepped up to serve the community. The Chiefs supplied fifty volunteer staff members to supplement the forty members of the election board on-site at Arrowhead Stadium. During election day, team president Mark Donovan was interviewed and shared that the process was incredibly efficient as well as spirited, noting that voters cheered at 6:00 a.m. as they entered the stadium.

And the team will continue to contribute to the community. As Super Bowl LV approached in four days, the Kansas City news outlets reported that Arrowhead Stadium is being considered for a mass vaccination site. "We stand ready," said team president Mark Donovan. Since that news broke, all NFL venues have agreed to participate as mass vaccination sites.

At Super Bowl LV, the NFL continued with the health and safety guidelines that were experienced throughout the 2020 season. Those efforts included only permitting approximately 22,000 fans to attend the game, including approximately 7,500 vaccinated health care workers as a show of thanks. The stadium was filled with cardboard cutouts of fans in all of the seats that were not sold, to both create the appearance of a full stadium and using those non-sold seats to provide the six-foot buffer between fans. Face mask use was required and appeared to receive compliance from the vast majority of fans. All in all, the game day environment inside the stadium provided a safe way to enjoy the game.

Looking forward, Jeff has just returned from Super Bowl LV and considers what is next: "Managing the facility security operations in the months before the vaccines are widely distributed is top of mind. Since the start of the pandemic in the US coincided with the beginning of the NFL fiscal year, we have completed almost one full cycle of all of our major events during pandemic circumstances. And we now have all events completed for the season. This will provide a template for us to use until the vaccines provide a return to a normal operating posture."

Reflecting on the past two seasons and the unique experience of doing it during the COVID-19 pandemic, Jeff noted, "We are fortunate to have won Super Bowl LIV in Miami on February 2, 2020, prior to the onset of the pandemic in the US. We had the ability to experience everything that the Super Bowl has to offer, including being crowned champions in a sold-out environment. I am thankful for that experience and proud to have earned a Super Bowl ring. I am even more proud of the resilience the NFL has demonstrated thus far in executing our season by carrying forth our protocols every day in the face of the pandemic."

CHAPTER 12

ALL ABOUT RELATIONSHIPS

Maureen Rush
Vice President for Public Safety and Superintendent of the Penn Police
Department
University of Pennsylvania

The University of Pennsylvania has a long-admired and world-class safety and security program on its campus nestled in University City, near downtown Philadelphia (the sixth largest city in the country). And that comes with its risks, including crime, traffic, violence, drug trafficking, and more. But Penn is an Ivy League–member school with current undergraduate tuition at nearly $80,000 per year. And this means their customers (students and their parents) demand a positive and safe environment.

And Penn is among the best at creating one.

Maureen Rush, the vice president for Public Safety and superintendent of the Penn Police Department, is a voice of calm, logic, and common sense. During her twenty-seven years at the university, she has built the highly regarded and resilient program that is in place today.

"What I heard when COVID-19 reached the University was how ready everybody felt."

And that is because they had a heck of a head start. The university started working with Kroll Associates on a crisis management program before 9/11. And 9/11 occurred while Penn's crisis management program was being stood up. Just seventeen days later, the anthrax terror mailing from a Princeton, New Jersey, mailbox (forty-five miles away) happened. Because it was a biologic threat, the decision was made to amplify the crisis management program to include both the hospital at the University of Pennsylvania and Presbyterian Hospital.

The Children's Hospital of Philadelphia (CHOP) is not owned by the university but sits squarely in the University City area, and so it was also included in the plan. The university and hospitals have often collaborated on safety and security planning and response. For example, the university and the three area hospitals had worked closely with the Department of Energy on a very high-level security plan for irradiators in the hospitals. They installed additional electronic access controls, alarms, and surveillance cameras for the labs where the irradiators are located.

Thus, the crisis management program was built with cross-functional expertise, professional and personal relationships, and real-world experiences. It has been relied upon since 2001, continuously updated and tested, and was solidly in place when the pandemic arrived.

Maureen explained, "About ten years later, 2011, we came to the realization that our mission or business continuity program should complement the crisis management program. So, the Mission Continuity program took on the same planning, tabletop exercises and interdependency planning as the Crisis Management program." For example, Penn's associate vice president of risk management brought their insurance brokers to the planning table to expand the ecosystem.

"Every year we run scenario exercises that include each school at the University (there are 12 unique under-graduate and graduate schools at Penn), and they go through this program. A lot of what we concentrated on during the Crisis and Mission Resilience planning and training are the very things being applied to manage the COVID-19 pandemic," said Maureen.

She continued, "It was super important to turn physical meetings and classes into virtual ones, fast." And the prior investments in IT infrastructure put the university in a strong position to make the shift. Online learning has been in the works for years and became vitally important to avoid a complete shutdown.

"The online learning platform was ready and with a few tweaks Penn was able to put most of its courses online. The exceptions included programs requiring in person learning, such as certain Dental and Nursing School classes or laboratory sessions," said Maureen.

The response during the 2001 anthrax threat demanded coordination and fast action across University City. All three area hospitals set up decontamination tents outside their emergency room entrances and hosed down exposed victims prior to entry into the hospital. That experience created muscle memory and resources in place, such as the tents, for responding to the pandemic. The hospitals were experienced and placed triage tents outside their three emergency rooms, providing the structure and process to test for COVID-19.

"We could not allow people who were positive with COVID-19 to enter the hospital. It is important to recognize that each of these pre-planned exercises took on a new life to manage the pandemic crisis. But the base was solid and supported adjustments for it to work," she said.

As news of the virus and its risk grew in February 2020, Penn utilized the Crisis Management Team (which was formed in 2001 under the Crisis Management Plan) led by the university president, executive vice president, and provost. It included senior leaders from each division, who led a subcommittee. And they were advised by Penn Medicine experts on medical issues such as infectious disease and vaccines.

Interestingly, the university was on spring break when COVID-19 infections spread broadly in March, and most students were not on campus. And the first major decision the Crisis Management Team faced was whether they should bring the students back to school.

"We made some decisions that not everyone was happy with. Universities are not typically top-down decision-makers, but this was not a moment for democracy. These decisions were made for the good of everyone," Maureen explained.

And Penn announced that "if you are not currently on campus, then Do Not Come Back. Stay Where You Are."

That worked for students living in the college dorms as they could be locked out of the university-owned buildings. But students from international locations or facing hardships needed exceptions to stay. Also, nearly 70 percent of Penn's students live off campus in non-university-owned apartments and have signed leases. Many considered those apartments their homes, and they returned to the University City area.

As the response to the pandemic evolved, Penn created and communicated exception rules that allowed for some to stay on campus while those living off campus would be required to stay off campus. For example, the school designated one dorm with five hundred beds for quarantine and announced only students living on campus in student housing would have access. While the university would help off campus students in need of testing or treatment, they would have to quarantine in their apartments, not the quarantine dorm.

Compliance with new rules related to gatherings, social distancing, and curfews were put in place. It fell to the Penn Police, who were on the front line of breaking up gatherings and parties, to ensure compliance. For the most part, students were well-behaved and compliant with the new rules.

"There were a couple of outliers, as always, and they were put in front of the student compact board for review and sanctions. And people would decide if their actions were a mistake of the head or a mistake of the heart," shared Maureen.

Penn also made the decision to not publicly share the number of expelled students. "We feel that the Student Compact is between Penn and the Student," said Maureen. Penn does summarize overall violations and related activity on its website for transparency (Compact Violation Consequences [upenn.edu]).

While Maureen heard how ready everyone felt they were to manage this crisis, she was impressed by how truly prepared the institution was to make the snow day decisions and execute the crisis management plan.

"Penn truly met the technology needs of the remote educational and working conditions. I think the Mission Continuity planning that was put in place paid off. And that started when Hurricane Katrina hit Tulane University. We studied what that looked like, what it would mean if we were completely shut down as Tulane was. How do people continue to work, deliver classes, pay the bills, make payroll? And we learned from that crisis how to prepare. We were in a remarkable spot when this started. And that gave us the foundation from which to evolve our response," said Maureen.

All these changes in a time of crisis come with a cost, but Penn put the safety of its stakeholders first.

"And budget went out the window," said Maureen.

As the leader for the Division of Public Safety, Maureen is among eight key division leaders that report to the executive vice president, overseeing the operational, financial, and physical initiatives of the university.

Maureen shared, "It is called a crisis for a reason. All the planning and decision-making on what we would or would not resource in the coming year became mute. As a team we focused on managing the pandemic and solving problems. It was clear there would be unknown costs. No one really knew how this was going to evolve, how long it would or will last, or its impact to our income and expenses. What was clear from our executive leadership was that the cost to stay in front of the pandemic thereby reducing the spread, illness and death in our community was paramount for our resilience and recovery. Doing the responsible thing is who we are. Responding requires action and those actions have a cost. The spending decisions were not made in a vacuum. Everything was presented, discussed and approved even if we did not know what the total cost would be. Clearly, these were not expenditures found in the current fiscal budget."

Penn is a well-run organization, and its fiduciary responsibility to its stakeholders remained as stable as possible as the pandemic continued through the year requiring additional spending to mitigate risks. All of the Mission Resilience decisions were approved while revenues declined. However, with a $15 billion endowment as of June 2020, there is a considerable but manageable disruption to the university's finances.

Having responded to the initial outbreak, the recovery phase continued.

"The next big job was and still is testing. Not only making test readily available, but mandating it in some cases. If contractors are entering buildings, they need to ensure they are tested and then are able to display a Green pass on their phone using the Penn Open Pass program. Some Penn staff and contractors are union members adding a level of negotiation to the process. But we worked out the policies and processes," Maureen said.

There is significant coordination to reopening the buildings. Research work continues, for example, and those operations had to be facilitated. A professor teaching from an empty classroom still requires support from IT, facilities, security, and access for educators. The IT online communications tools and cleaning and disinfecting requirements increase and require new resources. The Mission Resilience plan also required that COVID-19–specific signage in 150 buildings be created and placed.

"Nothing is one size fits all. If you have a good base you can pivot. COVID-19 is different than a typical crisis. COVID-19 keeps going and creates long term challenges. For example, most crises do not involve health related issues, but this one did and that led to engagement with Penn Medicine. And we were prepared for that from our experience with Anthrax. The Safety and Security team has been here every day since COVID-19 arrived supporting the community. And we have been hit by the virus and dealing with a reduced workforce," shared Maureen.

As the holidays and cold weather arrived in 2020, the predicted infections arrived too. About a week after the Thanksgiving holiday, nearly half of the safety and security team, including over 120 proprietary and 550 contract officers, started showing COVID-19 symptoms. That led to the Public Safety Division's adoption of the Penn Open Pass App to enter information about how they were feeling and receive an "enter" or "do not enter"—a facility message on your phone. Receiving the red, "do not enter" message locked you out of the facility.

The Security Operations Center (SOC) is your technology and communications hub. Your physical assets, such as weapons, are also secured there. And it is built for collaboration. Employees are constantly in close contact with others, and as a result, the community spread is fast.

Unless you have a virtual or remote security operations center in place, then moving or virtualizing a police department and command center is nearly impossible. The university's backup center near University City is logical for foreseen events such as a power outage or fire at the main facility. But a pandemic does not fit within that model because moving the infected or at-risk people a few miles away is not a solution.

"Although we have a PennComm Emergency Communications Center backup site across the river at the Pennovations Works center, we still had to operate police and security operations from our main headquarters. While we had PPE policies in place these people work closely together. The supervisors and detectives were the first to become infected," said Maureen.

With staffing level down, Penn Safety and Security adjusted to deliver vital services with fewer people by changing from three ten-hour shifts to two twelve-hour shifts. We hired a deep cleaning company to come in three times a day. That had two positive outcomes. First, less people and fewer shifts stopped the spread. Second, it gave our team confidence that they were safe.

"And that brings us to the next stage in our response plan, vaccinations," stated Maureen.

The University of Pennsylvania and the hospital at the University of Pennsylvania are steeped in medical expertise, personnel, and essential workers. The protocols and policies they have put in place will be followed, evaluated, and improved upon as feedback comes and guidance changes.

The first vaccinations went to the medical workers, essential personnel, and contractors who serve as essential personnel. And the hospital will be among the community resources providing vaccinations along CDC guidelines to the community.

Maureen explained, "Safety and Security is, by design, at the center of everything. Police, fire, security technology, the Penn Comm Center and the Helpline. We are center to all the 'stuff' that is going on. Our work is not in one area, so we have our hands in everything. In addition to helping with the students, we worked with bringing back the faculty and staff groups. We did this in stages by looking at each building; how many people did we need to support operations or run a class? The Crisis Management and Mission Continuity plans and team investments really paid off in preparing us to manage through the pandemic."

On Sunday, January 10, 2021, students began returning to Penn for the opening of the spring semester. They were greeted with new societal and compliance rules, including testing in an incredibly altered Philadelphia.

The Penn website homepage announces, "A Move In Like No Other," and a banner across the top brings users to the Penn Cares COVID-19 Response page, filled with both direction and resources communicating "Actions to keep the Penn Community healthy." This governs the continued opening of classes, even virtually, and is online at upenn.edu (Home | Coronavirus).

Within the plan are university alert levels from 1 to 4:

1. Baseline Mitigation Strategies
2. Heightened Awareness
3. Safer at Home
4. Campus Closure

Per the University's COVID-19 Website:

How the Alert Levels Are Determined

In making its determination, the COVID Response Team public health group reviews the following data on a daily basis, assessing the following factors as a group rather than individually:

- *Philadelphia weekly case counts.*
- *Asymptomatic test positivity (of faculty, staff, and students in the testing program).*

- *Symptomatic test positivity (of faculty, staff, and students in the testing program).*
- *Isolation and quarantine utilization and capacity for students.*
- *Change in 7 day rolling average case counts.*
- *Faculty/staff absenteeism.*

There are strong plans and process in place, but the challenges and demand for constant leadership and management are not over. Heavy snowstorms hit the Philadelphia area in early February, requiring both pandemic and weather responses to be intertwined. For example, testing facilities face weather-related interruptions, reducing or postponing testing. But the dining halls have to remain open because students cannot postpone eating.

Crisis management frameworks and plans have to be flexible, communicated, and resourced. And they require strong relationships, fast decision-making, and overcommunicating.

Maureen summarized, "This is the job. To serve the community, provide resilience and keep everyone as informed and safe as possible. And of course, the delivery of safety and security never takes a Snow Day!"

CHAPTER 13

SLACK'S GLOBAL RESILIENCE SOLUTION IS SLACK

Cary Monbarren
Global Manager—Physical Security / Safety / Business Resilience
Slack

Slack is an amazing success story, for, well, sort of a failure. Stewart Butterfield founded Flickr as an online game called Game Neverending. While the game didn't take off, the technology found success as a photo-sharing app bought by Yahoo in 2013. He then founded Tiny Speck, which created the online social game Glitch. But Glitch didn't succeed either. At least as a game. What they had actually built was a powerful productivity tool for business communications.

While online games were exciting, *Wired* magazine wrote, "On first blush, it sounds boring. Worse, it's a bit hard to explain because you haven't used anything like it before. It is a communications application, based on the system they created while building Glitch. It's called Slack."

And it wildly succeeded as a business software application, with Slack becoming a Silicon Valley unicorn.

Slack fundamentally changes how people collaborate internally and externally. Boring as that may be, Slack was valued at $1 billion by the end of its first year in business. And in the middle of the COVID-19 pandemic, as remote work became the new normal, Salesforce acquired the company for $27.7 billion. Not bad for a failed online game company.

This brief history is important to the story because Slack's Global Manager for Physical Security, Safety & Business Resilience, Cary Monbarren, not only uses Slack for internal security and resilience communications, but he also productized Slack for their customers as a go-to security and communications solution.

Slack channels can be created for any function, such as mass notification, alarms, alerts, or COVID-19 critical event management. And all the channels flow into the GSOC. The channels can be highly segmented by geography, specialty, or event. A fire alarm channel can be narrowed down to the stakeholders for a company's New York City office. That might include the GSOC, security leadership, and the local NYC fire station. If the office becomes unavailable, then a quick move to the "all NYC office" channel alerts a broader stakeholder set of the disruption and response plan. Crisis management commands are communicated through Slack channels to all who need to be included.

The additional cost for these services is zero for Slack's enterprise customers. Thus, Cary's story is unique in that he leads a security and resilience program with Slack as its platform. And it is similar as other enterprise security leaders in that the pandemic was the most disruptive event in modern business history.

Slack started monitoring reports of COVID-19 in mid-January and initiated the first review of their pandemic plan on January 30, 2020, when the World Health Organization (WHO) declared a Public Health Emergency of International Concern (PHEIC).

Because Slack is an online, software company, they were able to close all offices and move to a 100 percent remote workforce without losing productivity. And because they use their own product for communications and project management, their employees and connected partners experienced very little change in their workflow and behavior.

"We were in a unique position as a company, because our product was developed as a collaboration tool and worked extremely well while we were operating in a remote environment," Cary said.

He explained, "A COVID task-force was created to discuss response strategy. The team initially consisted of representatives from Global Safety & Security, Legal, The People Team (HR), Workplace, and Internal Communications. Slack was our primary communications platform.

Initially, the 'COVID Core Team' met in person, but moved to video conferencing after the offices were shut down."

"Our initial Coronavirus channel was created on 2/25/20 to discuss possible cancellation of a global conference. We initially allowed voluntary WFH, but went 100% remote on 3/9/20. The original plan was to WFH until the end of the month, but as cases increased and schools closed it became evident that remote work would not be a short-term solution," said Cary.

All decisions regarding daily operations were discussed in Slack channels or in video meetings by the task force. Each member of the team was meeting with their counterparts in other organizations to benchmark and develop policies and procedures. With over two thousand employees and a global footprint, the company quickly relied on its intelligence resources to follow the COVID-19 pandemic and ensure stakeholder safety and business continuity.

"Initially we used opensource news and critical event management software from NC4. As the pandemic progressed, we had project managers assigned to compile data and produce reports for each region. I also met weekly with my counterparts from several other companies to benchmark our response," explained Cary.

NC4 is a subsidiary of Everbridge and has been renamed Risk Center. It is an intelligence gathering and alerting service that fuels enterprise SOCs with information for further analysis and inclusion in decision-making. For example, customers subscribing for a specific region will be alerted to a natural disaster that can physically disrupt a company's operations due to power failures or road closures.

While there was no shortage of information, processing it was challenging. Cary noted, "The pandemic was unusual in that we had too much and sometimes conflicting information to work through. It would be beneficial to have more AI and remote capability in our security systems to analyze all the data points.

"Analyzing the data for each of our regions to understand the situation on the ground required a coordinated team effort, as you were always trying to hit a moving target. In most instances, the COVID restrictions were implemented all the way down at the local level and were changing frequently.

"Our decisions will always be data driven. We brought together leaders representing multiple departments and stakeholders to assess the situations, options and make recommendations. Employee safety always took precedence.

"Our process was straightforward and worked well."

Slack's product allowed everyone to collaborate in the channel and communicate with each other individually or with the entire group. Most of the decisions were made in the channel, or during a video meeting, if necessary. C-suite representatives were on the task force and could communicate directly (and instantly) with any of the executive staff.

"Our initial plan was simply 'check the box' behaviors including stay home, wash your hands, wear a mask, etc., But, as the pandemic progressed, we identified other issues resulting from working remotely 100% of the time such as internet limitations and power outages, especially due to the 2020 fires in northern California," Cary said. Slack is headquartered in San Francisco.

"Slack is fortunate in that much of our work can be done anywhere online. For example, I can personally manage my entire GSOC from my cellphone through the Slack product. We did have other redundancies, such as mobile hotspots available for employees that needed them, and creating an allowance so employees could purchase upgraded internet plans for their home. Ultimately it comes down to ensuring the employees have cross training and can jump in to assist each other when required," shared Cary.

The security team absorbed the reception and workplace responsibilities that were previously managed by Slack employees. Cary explained, "For most of the pandemic the security organization has been the only personnel who are physically onsite."

As a soldier, Cary led a Weapons of Mass Destruction Civil Support Team (WMD-CST), and his training involved disaster response in austere environments. And it included pandemic planning. His military experience and expertise drew him into the added roles of assisting in the global reopening plans for each office.

"It was a challenge to ensure that all responses both met region specific guidelines and aligned with our company culture and values. We had multiple conversations internally regarding the protocols required to return to the office safely, and how comfortable we would be implementing them. Slack offices, and most of the technology companies in this area, are known for having a certain look and feel. It is one thing to reduce the number of amenities that are provided, such as the snacks or closing the espresso bar, but it's totally different when you're discussing temperature checks and enforcement of PPE and social distancing," Cary said.

Ultimately, Slack decided the best and safest course of action was to extend the work-from-home policy until they could fully return to their offices with the least amount of disruption.

"We have managed the pandemic threat by quickly shifting to working remotely. And we have stayed current on best practices and supporting our stakeholders with communications that addressed their wellness, not just their work," stated Cary.

To address the unique difference of a health crisis, Slack contracted with an MD to serve as the subject matter expert crafting their safe return-to-work plan for reopening offices.

"The upcoming challenges will be opening the offices and defining the 'new-normal.' We are still determining what percent of the company will remain remote and how many employees want to return to the office. This obviously affects how we manage access and respond to employee incidents. Even small things like the ergonomics program will be challenging in the hybrid work model," shared Cary.

Slack's corporate standard is to provide a sit/stand desk for all employees. The company also conducts regular ergonomics assessments on-site and has additional equipment available if needed.

"Obviously, most employees did not have these amenities when working from home. I've been in multiple video meetings where an employee was sitting on the floor, or wherever quiet place they could find, with their laptop on a pillow. This just exacerbated any current employee ergonomic issues and initiated problems for employees that were previously unaffected," said Cary. To address these new COVID-19-created challenges, Slack created an allowance for employees to purchase equipment. The company is in the process of onboarding a software solution for self-assessments and has hired a provider to conduct 1:1 virtual ergonomic assessments with their remote employees.

Cary and the global team are using Slack for all security and safety communications and collaboration, including the pandemic response. Because they know and use the product daily, using it enterprise-wide for crisis management was a natural action. And the crisis management experience will expand its use for security, safety, and resilience programs.

CHAPTER 14

Digital Transformation Drives Physical Security

Brian Tuskan
Senior Director, Chief Security Officer
Microsoft

Microsoft's annual revenue grew $18 billion during the COVID-19 pandemic year of 2020. Microsoft's business, like other technology companies, was purpose built for both a remote workforce and supporting customers requiring remote work environments.

In his letter to employees (and shared with the public) on March 21, 2020, Microsoft CEO Satya Nadella's noted the "countless examples of colleagues across the company stepping up to meet this challenge – both the challenge of their own circumstances and that of their customers" and expressed great empathy recognizing, "we are in uncharted territory." Most eye catching about his letter is the lengthy list of decisions, actions and accomplishments just ten days after the World Health Organization declared COVID-19 a pandemic.

Microsoft's products not only kept their employees productive when working remotely but enabled them to support customers that needed to shift operations to remote locations, such as helping schools shift to remote learning by providing free use of Microsoft Teams. The company also supported the medical response to the pandemic working with the CDC on a self-assessment tool and launched a COVID-19 vaccine management platform.

Among the leaders "stepping up to meet the challenge" was Brian Tuskan, Microsoft's CSO/senior director for global physical security operations across 190 countries and over 165,000 employees. His strong interest in technology made him a perfect fit for the world's biggest software company; he just celebrated his twentieth year at the company and was named the head of physical security in 2019.

As a student, he took computer courses when it was still very new and he recognized how technology improved productivity. He joined the Honolulu Police Department in 1989 and the Redmond Police Department in 1993 and became known as both computer savvy and adept at using data to identify statistical trends.

During his tenure at Microsoft, he was a team member that leveraged Microsoft's technology solutions and services to digitally transform their physical strategy leveraging the cloud, AI, and Machine Learning. Now leading the team responsible for physical security and safety of the company's people, property, and infrastructure, Brian is a key leader who helps protect the business.

Microsoft crisis management team leadership is within the Information Security group. This well-regarded program was named the Best Cyber Security Company in 2019 by Cybersecurity Insider's Cybersecurity Excellence Awards stating: *Microsoft's Crisis Management Program is best-in-class, including seven crisis management principles to prioritize response and a decision and guidelines matrix identifying the most critical decisions and associated owners. The seven principles are unique to Microsoft, as well as the focus placed on them by executive to drive response action and priorities. Microsoft's program is also differentiated by its scale – we serve a huge variety of customers and our crisis management program must be built to cover every hazard that could impact them. Customers include essential services like hospitals and first responders, so it is critical that we manage crisis response well.* (https://cybersecurity-excellence-awards.com/candidates/microsoft/)

"Our structure at Microsoft is different than other organizations for crisis management because we are a technology company, and our biggest risks are digital. The company has about 60-70 regional and country-level crisis management teams to execute responses for more typical local crises or events. Each has a business executive as Chair and leaders from operational departments including HR, Real Estate, Security, Finance, Legal sit on the committees. If the crisis is in a local or regional area, that team manages the incident. Of course, the pandemic was a global crisis, and the Enterprise Crisis Management team took the lead on the company's response. The regional and country-level teams supported the global decisions."

The crisis management teams hold regular table-top exercises at the global and local levels. Each crisis management team has at least one per year. The training on policies, technology, and processes creates relationships, improvements, and muscle memory. The member's expertise and experience kicked in immediately to enable ongoing operations and continued resilience.

"As a global company with significant business in China, we became aware of the virus in December 2019 in Wuhan, China. I learned of it through the news and from our regional security leader in China, Peter Qi." Because the onset of COVID-19 coincided with the Chinese New Year, Mr. Qi was on vacation in a coastal area. Leveraging technology's power and flexibility, he managed the pandemic response for physical security remotely and did not return home to Beijing for nearly four months.

As the first US case was confirmed near Seattle, Washington, on January 13, 2020, Brian was heading to San Diego for the annual International Security Management Association Conference. "I am an ISMA member and attended the conference in late January. They changed the planned schedule, which caught everyone's attention, bringing Dr. Peter Druckman to present on the pandemic. That created a scary buzz at the event that the virus was both coming to the United States and going to have a significant, global impact."

"I know our life safety, and travel program support had to prepare for the pandemic's impact, beyond our normal activity levels. Some countries were starting to restrict international travel, which meant our employees could be stuck outside their home country. We worked on solving for that possibility. Tracking all the different government agencies quarantining regulations would be complex. We had our analysts and operations teams create a picture of the scope and scale of pandemic regulations." They incorporated and followed CDC, WHO, and various country, state, and city guidelines into the travel programs and advisories.

Our global security analysts gathered and synthesized this information for operations teams to identify the best options, decide on the best action and communicate it at the local or appropriate level.

"I recall being at a Microsoft leadership training program around March 5th (2020) with about 35 colleagues. We held what was then a normal meeting with some workshops and typical close contact during the program. The next night Microsoft announced all employees would start working remotely." One death had been reported in the United States by March 6, 2020, but Microsoft reviewed the risk of the pandemic spreading and its capacity to operate successfully with a remote workforce. (^CDC COVID Data Tracker)

The pandemic became "very real" for Brian when the Life Care Center Nursing Home COVID-19 spread made local and then national news. Brian lives near the Kirkland, Washington, area, where the facility is located. It is also close to the Microsoft campus. It was identified as an early center of the outbreak in the United States as thirty-seven people died, and nearly 70 percent of the employees and residents tested positive for the coronavirus ("Nursing Home Linked to 37 Coronavirus Deaths Faces Fine of $600,000," *New York Times*, www.nytimes.com).

"Our role in global security shifted to the pandemic response. In my role, many of the global security team and I are part of the Crisis Management Team as subject matter experts for physical security. And in response to the pandemic, the things we had to think about and manage included how to lock down buildings and ensure they were safe. If essential employees were entering the buildings, we needed to have a program ensuring both the buildings and people were safe."

The security team also leveraged resources, such as the Overseas Advisory Council (OSAC), for updated travel restrictions and support to get employees back to their home countries. "The best description is that we were well organized, and our crisis management plans kicked and worked through what was a chaotic and difficult situation. No one had been through a pandemic situation before, and with the travel shutdowns, people were just stuck. And we worked to help them get back home."

"From a security perspective, locking down a facility with access control and maintaining situational awareness through video is straightforward. It did not require increased manpower. We have robust contingency plans for our technology and relied on those. We have two VSOCs (virtual security operations centers) in Redmond, Washington, and Hyderabad, India. Both have failover, so if one goes down, the other can manage globally. The operators have "go bags," including laptops in case they need to evacuate and work from outside the facility; they can run the operation remotely."

"And that is precisely what happened in Hyderabad. When India shut down, our workers were not allowed to travel to the office buildings. At the same time, we had to reduce the Redmond staff to a skeleton crew to ensure social distance for COVID-19 safety. I also have to recognize the real estate team that continuously cleaned and disinfected our facilities where the essential workers perform critical roles. That both kept everyone safe and created confidence that the workplace was indeed safe."

"Microsoft global security has been working on a digital transformation strategy moving our platform to the cloud, SaaS, and virtual environments. And we are doing it with "COTS" (commercial off-the-shelf technology) and not relying on specialized or customized technology solutions. That work positioned us well to ensure security's availability and resilience during the pandemic crisis response."

Because many security team members work virtually by the nature of their roles, moving to an all-virtual workflow was seamless, speeding the response. "We use Microsoft Teams regularly as our communications platform, and everyone was well versed in how to use it in this fully remote environment."

The security team proved it was truly a team. "Some of our departments, such as security operations, were incredibly busy and needed additional resources. But others, such as investigations, were less busy. With the facilities closed, their workload was reduced. And we were able to share resources across the departments. Our events security team became completely available and were able to assist the operations and analysts' teams. We have a deep bench and the flexibility to work through the crisis as a team. Investigators were able to snap in as analysts to research governmental sites on country closures and risk updates as the situation changed daily. The event security team assisted our security operations teams to sit on critical crisis management meetings providing depth so that others could get adequate rest.

There is no doubt that the pandemic was a stress test for crisis management and resilience programs everywhere. "We were fortunate that Microsoft's program was mature and able to scale." Brian's experience recognizes that not only was the response to the pandemic a marathon and not a sprint but building a mature organization was also a marathon.

"As I look at the experience, it is clear that years of strategy, preparation, and investment in physical security, from technology to hiring the right people to training, worked. Yes, there were extra work hours for everyone, but that is to be expected. More importantly, our ability to move to a virtual platform and put all the planning to the test and have it work is rewarding.

"Just because you can work 24/7 at a remote location does not mean that you should. I communicated to our team to factor in downtime, even to schedule breaks between remote meetings. It sounds unusual, but it is possible to schedule 10-12 hours of meetings without a break and not even realize how long a day you just had until the last one ends. So, we worked to be proactive with scheduling in breaks, hours, and an end to people's workday.

"I learned how fragile life is, too. When this first arrived, and I looked at the projections for infections and deaths, I was just astounded they were projecting 200,000 deaths in the US, and now we are at 500,000. To realize how many people died in the past year, and my heart goes out to people who lost loved ones to the virus. And I have a profound respect for essential front-line workers. I also have a different take on what is important. We used to be very formal during video meetings from remote locations. Now hearing the dog bark or a child in the background is very human, OK, and in many ways, better. The relationship and collaboration are important; the brief interruption is not."

CHAPTER 15

A MARATHON, NOT A SPRINT

Jack Sullivan, Global Chief Security and Resiliency Officer—Vice President
Boston Scientific

Jack is, perhaps, the most metrics- and measurement-driven executive in the corporate security profession. When we first met, Jack was the director for Corporate Security and Loss Prevention at Dunkin' Brands, which owns the Dunkin' Donuts and Baskin-Robbins restaurants. And he had an interesting and challenging job—sell the option of paying for better security to franchisees.

He stated at the time, "Our primary goal with the franchisee is to reduce theft, increase profitability and improve financial performance." And that was successfully done with metrics, by showing an uptick in performance to the level that the cost of the program (insurance, so to speak) more than paid for itself as not only would the franchisee capture the lost fraud revenue, often the performance of that store would increase beyond just the money stolen. Jack's data-driven programs created high value for Dunkin' Brands, its franchised stores, and the security team.

Jack was one of the first people I met to present security in the dollars and cents that helped his internal business customers both understand its value and choose to spend money for it. It is understandable why the COVID-19 pandemic is especially vexing to his way of thinking: "There is no answer in place for beating the pandemic right now, which means it is really hard to bring shape to the solution. The focus is on minimizing its impact until there is a resolution through vaccinations and herd immunity. But that is not satisfying."

After Dunkin' Brands, he joined Starbucks as the Chief Security Officer / Vice President–Global Resilience, Safety and Security in Seattle, with similar vision and impact. In 2017, he returned home to Massachusetts, joining Boston Scientific to build the world-class security and resilience program. Boston Scientific is a global medical device manufacturer dedicated to transforming lives through innovative medical solutions. Like many multinationals, they have complex distribution and supply chains that need to continue to operate in order to bring their lifesaving devices to patients.

> After receiving an email about a quickly spreading virus in from one our intelligence analysts protecting operations in China, our team mobilized to protect our employees and operations.

> We immediately moved to protect our operations to mitigate spread and protect employees We purchased thermal cameras to assess employees before admitting them to the buildings. We established criteria with our China business leaders to limit the spread and agreed that reaching those metrics would trigger office closures.

Boston Scientific put policies in place to limit the virus's spread. They restricted their employees' travel between Asia and the United States before the first case was recorded in Washington state.

> We knew the pandemic was coming to the US, but we didn't know how severe it would be or certainly become. We restricted travel globally and started monitoring break outs, and we could see its start, seven cases in Japan, then four cases in Singapore before exploding in Italy.

At Starbucks, Jack developed a pandemic management plan due to his interest in the mathematic concept of herd immunity, but never thought he would actually experience one in his career, explaining his interest and knowledge in R naught values. The R_0, or R naught value, the calculation of the average "spreadability," of an infectious disease was highly concerning. "Based on how contagious COVID-19 is, if you see 7 cases, the reality is that you probably have 500."

Boston Scientific knew the virus would spread quickly and started thinking about their manufacturing plant in Asia. "The workers are close together and if one person is infected, then what would that mean to the rest of the people? That is when we started taking temperatures."

They also began a strong communications effort explaining to employees that if they did not feel well, to please not come to work. Explaining candidly that they would not be looked upon poorly. The company wanted them, their coworkers and their families, to be healthy. Other measures such as social distancing and staggered shifts were also put into place.

And while Boston Scientific, like many businesses, did not have a specific pandemic management plan, his team had rehearsed their corporate crisis management protocols several times in the prior year. What worked was having a team that had successfully managed crises before. "You identify and plan for the five things that are most likely to significantly disrupt your business while not going down every rabbit hole."

Pandemics did not make that list at most companies (but they may in the future).

> By having a strong team and plan for those most likely risks, such as an earthquake or political unrest that will disrupt supply chains, travel or business function, then 80% of that can be applied to the pandemic. By having the bulk of the structure for response in place and then customizing the other 20% to the specific threat, you are in a strong starting position.

When COVID-19 arrived in the United States, the security and resilience team had already been working on COVID matters for several months. They knew each other and, importantly, each other's personalities. They had crisis communication protocols and escalation points in place, so when an event reached a trigger point, it was raised to the next leadership level.

> The habit of getting together at the C-suite level with legal, HR, IT, finance, etc., and walking through how we would

handle a crisis created familiarity. And that put us ahead
of the pandemic response.

After the alert about China, Security and Resilience met with the C-suite on a daily basis. First the meetings were focused on the response in China and, by late January, the US and the rest of their global footprint. "Initially, we met daily with the C-suite and it expanded to include the people that owned the workstreams. You must marshal the efforts against the workstreams to ensure the response is synchronized and efforts are not duplicated. You have to be super-efficient because if more than one person is working on the same thing, that can really cost you time in a crisis."

Having great communications throughout the enterprise ensured a more successful response. Jack also relied on his background as a Marine as the one thing that has most helped him.

> This had the familiar combat feel at the start. There was
> a battle rhythm on how to attack COVID-19, the enemy,
> if you will. The intensity of the action as the virus spread
> and the crisis grew was battle-like. And being the person
> that could not fade into the background and wither was
> familiar. The job is to rise to the occasion.

Several of Jack's veteran colleagues shared that they felt their PTSD rising, and he related, "I could feel mine spiking too."

The similarities—that COVID-19 is the enemy, it is invisible, and there is no cure or vaccine—could create a sense of hopelessness after a while. "All you can do is keep people safe by having them stay at home, give them PPE and educate them. But having my security team on the front line of the response is also familiar to combat experience."

His Marine training, to be ready for combat by enduring tremendous pressure, built confidence that he could manage through the situation. "There were a few times I wanted to crawl under the bed," he laughs, "But I cannot do that. I stayed in the fight."

An initial challenge was acquiring the right kind of masks for the workforce. Demand was high, supply low, and quality uncertain. "It felt like everyone was trying to buy the same ten masks. Boston Scientific uses masks in manufacturing, but not the kind needed for preventing viral spread. This is not an area security and resilience had much experience in, but we worked on it and figured it out.

"We would request and receive samples that met our specifications only to place the bulk order and receive a different, lower quality product." Jack also leveraged relationships from his special operations tenure to connect the team with additional PPE sources.

"We have some pretty smart people and they created a good process, engaged our supply chain and indirect sourcing teams and acquired PPE."

Next, they acquired testing services for the company. "We identified different solutions that fit the needs for different work environments including manufacturing plants, work from home, and employees who work in the field, including hospitals." The goal was to make the tests as frictionless as possible for the employee as early tests were difficult to use. Due to the large population of employees working from home, they could be quite precise in who was offered tests. During the year, testing solutions have evolved to be both easier to use and to see the results more rapidly. Boston Scientific's culture as a medical technology company and its policies may have contributed to achieving infection rates below those in their communities. Regular temperature screenings and health inquiries may have also influenced safer behavior outside work environments.

The company made other changes to reduce risk, including increased air exchange in its facilities, and enacted other environmental changes. In hindsight, one of the team's biggest wins was to get leadership buy-in to suspend activity at global manufacturing sites in April, once they had determined that critical inventory and patient care would not be negatively impacted. Using a lesson learned from a deployment in Iraq, one of Jack's team members recalled a glass factory that was forced to do an emergency shutdown. "The factory had shut down immediately due to a local threat, and the liquid glass froze in the pipes—basically ruining the facility." The intent was not to wait for a community outbreak at a Boston Scientific site and be forced into an emergency shutdown. Rather, shutting down in a deliberate fashion allowed them to take a couple of weeks to design and train the team on safety protocols across the network and bring the sites back up safely. The program allowed manufacturing to continue through the worst moments of the pandemic without any internal-community-spread events.

While providing resilience response across the global company, it is important to recognize that COVID-19 was not the only crisis the company has been dealing with.

There have been terrible fires in California requiring us to get employees out of harm's way. And we have significant operations in Minneapolis where there was protest activity over the summer requiring additional resources to make sure the labor force could get to work safely, and that manufacturing would continue.

The pandemic has had a greater impact on supply chains than a discrete event such as weather, fire, or terror have had in the past. "These events happen, and you move forward. But COVID-19 was unraveling more every single day. You have to deal with the disease in the moment, what is actually happening on that day, and plan for the future. It is tough to do both."

One of the significant learnings and changes is the reality that people can get burned-out.

The 24-7 response and drawn-out length of the pandemic has been tough on the Boston Scientific security team (as well as other departments). "It is not easy. The day job is tough, and the subject matter is not exactly uplifting. This is a grim task and the volume is massive. Those things you look forward to are kind of ethereal. On the positive side, we are starting to track vaccinations and see a return toward normal this year." At the time of our interview, the US had vaccinated about 2 percent of the population.

"People are fried. And this was not an issue we had to deal with in the past. The longevity and uncertainty of the crisis response has had and continue to have an impact on the quality of life. When a person is both working in it and living it, it just burns them out after a while. Telling someone to take time off for four days and that we really do not want to hear from them was new. And we implemented it to protect our team." One thing to note here is the vast array of mental health support Boston Scientific offered to its employees. Caring is a core value of the company, and COVID has been a great opportunity to put that core value into action through various programs offered by their Human Resources team, including counseling and flexibility on work scheduling.

The Security and Resilience team received tremendous support from two critical areas. First, they worked with an internal team of biostatisticians to build predictive models on the virus's spread and impact. Second, those were presented to Jack's boss, the EVP of Operations, who was the snow day decision-maker for the company. "He would review our recommendations, ask great questions and send us back to work. He was on every crisis management call and fully supportive of our work."

The Boston Scientific Resilience and Security team is the same size and shape today as it was when the pandemic arrived. "We built a great team at a high level and they responded beautifully. They rose to the occasion during this particular event and worked many more hours, but we are now returning to a more normal work life balance. No doubt this team would be able to quickly scale back up if needed. I am getting very positive feedback on the work they have done." Among the unique aspects of the team are project managers who do not have security experience. They bring a different discipline to the team that helps organize and move projects forward.

Reflecting on the future and the changes this experience is bringing, Jack notes that based on the work the team delivered on regarding that pandemic that the team has unprecedented visibility within the larger organization and that they are being pulled into many new work streams to offer their unique perspective. "My expectation is that our name will swap from 'security and resilience' to 'resilience and security' as the work our team has done has moved the impression of our service from 'guns, guards and gates' to enabling the business to be more impervious to disruptions, such as disasters, geo-political risk or even pandemics. Resilience is a positive notion in that it keeps the business operating, contributing to its economic security. As a result, security should logically move under the 'Resilience' umbrella."

Jack, who never sits still, plans to expand his focus on risk and resilience. "Recording what did and didn't go well when it is still fresh in our memory is important. I want to address any departmental issues, educate our team and myself to improve the program.

"Being stronger and more resilient can give Boston Scientific an advantage against competitors that are neither prepared nor able to sustain through negative events that impact business operations."

CHAPTER 16

THE HUMAN IN US ALL

Dr. Park Dietz
Founder and President
Threat Assessment Group

"Before the pandemic, it could be said accurately, up to about half the working people in America have a diagnosable mental disorder in a given year," began Park Dietz, MD, MPH, PhD, who is the founder and president of Threat Assessment Group, the leading provider of workplace violence prevention services for large corporations and law firms. He is perhaps better known for Park Dietz & Associates, his expert witness company that has participated in highly publicized legal cases, including John Hinckley Jr., Milwaukee cannibal Jeffrey Dahmer, the Unabomber Ted Kaczynski.

His experience working with employers and employees is insightful for the mental and emotional impact crises, in general, and the COVID-19 pandemic, in particular, have on employees.

"Now, what does that mean?" he began to unpack his statement. "We have a lot of diagnoses and they vary greatly in severity. So, it is easy to mislead with that percentage. It means that about 50% of American workers have a diagnosable mental disorder in a given year including every kind of substance abuse, sleeping disorder, anxiety, warped personality, and more."

There is a lot of overlap among these categories because research shows if a person has one mental disorder, then they are more likely to have a second or third.

"People can do whatever they wish with statistics, but my point is that even without the pandemic, lots of people suffer to one extent or another with what could be diagnosed as a mental disorder. And mental disorders include many kinds of emotional problems such as anxiety and depression." Additionally, cognitive difficulties such as those that occur during recovery for many COVID-19 patients or in dementia are considered mental disorders.

And the list is substantial. The Diagnostic and Statistical Manual of Mental Disorders (DSM–5) is published by the American Psychiatric Association. Their website describes it as the standard classification of mental disorders used by mental health professionals in the United States and is a product of more than ten years of effort by hundreds of international experts in all aspects of mental health. It was first published in 2013.

DSM-5 is 991 pages long.

Stressful situations and trauma can cause symptoms that may meet the criteria for diagnosis of a mental disorder. Trauma has been heavily studied, and over time, the definitions have been changed. Before 2013, a diagnosis of posttraumatic stress disorder (PTSD) required a threat to bodily integrity of the person experiencing the event, but since 2013, DSM-5 has recognized a broader range of events as sufficient to cause PTSD.

> The way to think about the reaction to stress and trauma, without getting hyper technical, is that everyone is vulnerable to being affected by stressful life events and traumatic events. The border between stress and trauma is quite fuzzy. Some types of stressful events are so severe that everyone would agree to name it a trauma.

Thinking about the effects of trauma has expanded to include secondary trauma, which is a trauma a person only heard about as described directly by a victim. But secondary trauma can result in the onset of mental symptoms.

"This distinction is illustrated by the difference between a person highly distressed by learning of a loved one being harmed versus being harmed oneself. The distinction is between a vicarious experience and a personal experience," explained Dr. Dietz. Increasing attention is being paid to the symptoms and mental health needs of first responders, including health care and social service professionals who repeatedly deal with trauma victims; and Dr. Dietz pointed out that similar concerns should be addressed with those security and human resources professionals who routinely engage with victims of workplace threats and bullying and with employees affected by intimate partner violence.

This is sometimes referred to as secondary trauma. It occurs when a person is speaking directly with victims of trauma and hearing about trauma repeatedly. And it has been increasingly recognized that first responders and others exposed to this kind of secondary trauma develop their own symptoms, suffering, and changes to their view of the world.

Secondary trauma and its resultant toll on first responders and health care professionals whose work involves caring for the pandemic's direct victims is a legacy of the COVID-19 pandemic, the ultimate toll of which is not yet known. And the professional community is just beginning to identify ways to help people facing chronic, secondary trauma.

Thus, psychiatry's and psychology's understanding of trauma has been expanded over time as humans and their response to it have been studied.

Moreover, the effects on people who learn of traumatic events and crisis only through the media are attracting greater attention and study. As Dr. Dietz explained, "We now recognize that many of the same symptoms that occur when an individual personally experiences a traumatic event, such as intrusive recollections, being unable to stop thinking of the event, or having nightmares about it, can occur when one's exposure to the event was not personal or even through the vicarious experience of a loved one or victims one has attended to, but also through media exposure alone which occurred after 9/11 when large numbers of Americans nowhere near the crash sites developed symptoms." The 9/11 attack was seen by many on television, usually repeatedly; but in 2001, social media and video streaming were far less available than today. Dr. Dietz suggested that while data have not yet been collected on the effects of remote viewing of the riots of 2020 and the breach of the Capitol in January of 2021, he would expect these events to have worsened the widespread symptoms of anxiety and depression already attributable to the COVID-19 pandemic and the political and media handling of it.

The stress and trauma impact and implications of 9/11 have been widely studied.

> It was discovered that a high percentage of New Yorkers developed symptoms even if they were not near Ground

Zero. And a surprisingly high percentage of Americans developed symptoms even though they were not near the New York City area. That led to a rethinking of how distressing and symptom-producing a televised event can be to the viewer.

These studies led Dr. Dietz to recommend in various forums that people reduce their self-exposure to distressing events by not repeatedly viewing them on various media such as the news.

While the word *trauma* has been diluted when people speak of a stressful or traumatic event that was not, by definition, putting them directly in harm's way, there is no dispute that people can develop symptoms and problems from indirect or vicarious exposure to stressful events.

Different people have different vulnerability levels, and it is not always clear how one will react in the face of stress. It is not known why some people take stress worse than others or why they are more resilient.

"There is significant attention being given to the issues of resilience and recovery as well as providing needed help and attention to those facing exposure to stress in reality or virtually. And while workers experience varying levels of stress across different industries and job duties, the professional help provided to affected workers across different industries is also quite uneven," said Dr. Dietz.

To demonstrate the broad differences in mental health services, Dr. Dietz shared this example: "It is clear that there are sizeable proportions of first responders exposed to great danger and to suffering, injury, disfigurement, and death but who get little to no support or help to cope with such exposure. In contrast, there are a few classes of workers whose employers provide them massive support, as occurs for some of the content moderators working to monitor and screen the images appearing on social media platforms.

"Receiving the help to be resilient and recover from these stressful exposures depends on which way the litigation gate swings. If an industry has experienced successful or reputation-damaging lawsuits for the emotional distress of its workers, companies in the industry take note and are more likely to scramble to provide the needed help.

"If an industry has immunity from such civil suits (as may occur for military, fire, and law enforcement agencies) or if nobody has been sued yet, it is far less likely that an investment will be made to proactively help those exposed to stress, whether they are direct front line workers or those exposed through images."

Investing in people to identify human vulnerabilities and their tolerance to stress, and identifying ways to mitigate the threat of trauma, is no different than the physical and cybersecurity risk programs businesses employ. Choosing a predictive posture for workers exposed to high levels of stress versus reacting to negative events resulting from that exposure are ultimately economic and societal decisions.

In addition to the mental health impact on first responders, especially the security and safety workers focused on keeping their stakeholders safe, there is an unknown and still-to-be-measured toll for other employees, as Dr. Dietz detailed:

> The impact on employees is becoming clear. Not all measures are adequate and there are a lot of missing data points, but among those employees who are still employed and working remotely during the pandemic, the research points to these imperfectly understood findings:
>
> There is increased anxiety for almost everyone for a whole host of reasons. From their personal experience to concern for family members, the inability to handle an invisible hazard is highly stressful. In addition, not having control of certain outcomes including remaining employed, economic uncertainty, or becoming ill.
>
> There is also an increased use of substances, even during working hours, as an inappropriate coping mechanism. That includes increased use of alcohol, marijuana, and other drugs.
>
> Domestic violence has increased. Survivors who used to go to work are now at home. Work was a safe haven during the day, and now they are stuck at home with their abuser. The stress of this constant threat is a very big issue.
>
> Depression has increased during the pandemic, and I expect we will witness an increase in suicides. There

are increased calls to suicide hotlines now. But data on suicides is reported about 1 to 2 years later, and the actual impact will not be known until those data are available.

So, if I had to bet on what the mental health effects of the pandemic have been, I would bet on those four.

The Threat Assessment Group was founded in 1987 and is an outgrowth of Dr. Dietz's unique combination of practical and research experience in injury prevention, the analysis of threatening communications, mental disorders, and criminal behavior. He provides an unsettling analysis of the pandemic's true impact and costs:

> Prior to the pandemic's arrival and impact, we were actively researching the cost of various mental illness and behavioral issues to employers. The national data were inadequate for many of the problems we sought to measure. But, when we looked specifically at absenteeism and turnover as a result of a small number of problems: anxiety, substance abuse, depression, domestic violence, and bullying, we found reliable, national data.

> I can tell you that the costs of only absenteeism and turnover due to these five mental health and behavioral issues is staggering. And that's prior to the arrival of the pandemic! Nothing else has impacted every single American for an entire year as COVID-19 has. And the costs have yet to be understood and realized.

> The cost of training and early intervention to prevent and mitigate these risks is a pittance compared to the cost of not addressing the problems, and many of the costs of remediation are already being paid through underutilized employee assistance programs.

One group that is working to gain attention to the trauma leveled by the pandemic and get needed support is first responders. The hospital settings where they are working with COVID-19 patients are overwhelmed, overrun, and working extremely long hours. Sometimes they are separated from their families in quarantine to avoid spreading possible exposure.

"Being praised at a sporting event is nice. But it's not the support they need every day," noted Dr. Dietz.

The Heroes Act of 2020 took a step in that direction with financial support defining "qualified first responders" capable of receiving federal financial assistance as physicians, nurses, pharmacists, law enforcement officers, corrections officers, firefighters, emergency medical technicians, or paramedics who provide services in a county that has at least one confirmed case of COVID-19." But it does not clearly provide mental health services.

During my research, several participants stated that their experience in the military best prepared them for leading their organization's COVID-19 crisis management response. As Dr. Dietz explained, both the wartime and the COVID-19 experiences include facing uncertainty at their root.

> Those who faced battle in the military have an adaptive advantage. They faced uncertainty in the theater of war and upon facing it against the pandemic they are able to buckle down, not be distracted, and focus on the mission to the point of exhaustion. They are capable of managing their own emotions. The same thing happens with first responders in emergency rooms and police and fire departments.

Every first responder, chief security and resilience officer, and government health care worker faces an uphill challenge in their profession. They have chosen to protect people who often do not act in their own self-interest. They may not define themselves as being risk-takers, but their behavior is not risk averse.

Humans are hardwired and not likely to change their perception and tolerance of risk. Humans overeat, are overweight, drink too much alcohol, smoke cigarettes, abuse drugs, do not exercise enough, and text while driving. Workers flaunt safety compliance in hard hat, earplugs, safety vest, or steel-toe boots only in work areas.

These precautions are the result of trial and error (well, trial and injury) leading to identifying a better or safer way to work. The goal is to reduce further, future injuries to employees. But the human in many of us pushes back on the safety measures designed for their safety.

Working 24-7 to protect stakeholders that do not wish to be protected is a very difficult, if not infuriating, profession. And the COVID-19 pandemic exemplified this to the highest levels. People have different levels of risk tolerance, as well. The higher a person's anxiety, the more fearful they are and the more risk averse. Those who might be considered "fearless" by observers tend to be high risk-takers. One's fear and perception of risk can also be rapidly altered by certain medications or drugs, such as alcohol.

The pandemic crisis is projected to claim 630,000 lives in the United States by this book's publication in June 2021. The advice from the medical community to wear a mask, socially distance, and wash hands regularly was not only dismissed by many, but taken as a challenge to rebel against.

The mental and emotional risk tolerance of individuals who either did not believe the COVID-19 virus was a threat to them personally, for whatever reason, added to the challenges crisis management response teams faced and managed. Most of the participants shared that their organizations followed the science and included PPE as part of the enterprise's policy. Those that refused to comply explicitly or repeatedly were terminated from employment, expelled from campus, or barred from the premises.

This exacerbated the stress put upon the crisis management teams who repeatedly addressed compliance due to employee behavior.

On the other side of the spectrum, people who are highly risk averse are skeptical that the COVID-19 vaccine is safe and may delay or reject being vaccinated. The ironic outcome of which is placing oneself in a high-risk situation due to one's low risk tolerance. Enterprise risk management teams included corporate communications from the outset, promoting the personal benefit of new safety policies and encouraging compliance.

Dr. Dietz summarized our conversation, "We have always presented our work as an early warning system for behavioral problems and mental health disorders. We operate under the belief that if everyone is trained and twenty people observe and recognize the signs, then at least one person will report it. And this early warning system results in mitigating threats and providing people with help. It works very well. But it is a hard sell. Which is why so much time and money is spent reacting to crises at a much higher human and financial cost than preventive measures."

III. RESILIENCE MANAGEMENT: STRATEGIES, TECHNOLOGIES, AND RECOVERY

CHAPTER 17

A DIFFERENT KIND OF CRISIS

One lesson I've learned is that if the job I do were easy, I wouldn't derive so much satisfaction from it. The thrill of winning is in direct proportion to the effort I put in before. I also know, from long experience, that if you make an effort in training when you don't especially feel like making it, the payoff is that you will win games when you are not feeling your best. That is how you win championships, that is what separates the great player from the merely good player. The difference lies in how well you've prepared.

—Rafael Nadal in Rafa

There are many books, consultants, classes, and professional certifications for critical event management providing expert advice for planning and executing a crisis management program. It is not the goal of this chapter to repeat those prescriptions for a fully funded and functional program. Because that is not the way crisis management response unfolded during the COVID-19 pandemic.

Enterprises for years have hired large consulting firms to come in and prepare detailed resiliency plans which included crisis management, business continuity plans, incident management protocols and disaster recovery/ business resumption plans. They consistently produced *encyclopedic documents that met the requirements of checking the box for management and the regulatory compliance folks. Once completed, these "plans" would sit on a shelf gathering dust and rarely were the covers even cracked. The huge liability problem that evolved out of this methodology of ensuring resiliency of the enterprise is that when the proverbial S**t Hit the Fan and an actual crisis or major incident occurred, no one followed the plans stated processes and requirements.*

One only has to look at a couple of cases like BP's Deepwater Horizon disaster to envision the significant liability that an enterprise has to weather when a crisis or major incident occurs and either the plan is inaccurate or significantly outdated or the prescribed processes in the plan are not followed. The elements of a solid resiliency plan are frankly not that complex and can be handled with simple yes-no decision trees; a few check lists and a few process flow charts. The old adage of "A Picture is Worth a Thousand Words" applies to the full scope of resiliency. With the addition of incredible new tools that allow designated management personnel to manage a crisis or any other type of incident directly from the palm of their hand via a smart phone."

Lynn Mattice
Former CSO of Three Major Global Corporations

This summary is based on a series of very honest and, for the most part, upbeat conversations with security, resilience, and safety executives on their experience during the pandemic. Despite not having dedicated budget or staff specifically for a health pandemic, the underlying crisis management planning, expertise, and training resulted in positive outcomes that enabled the enterprises to be resilient and remain operational, while supporting the health and safety of their stakeholders.

The pandemic showed the strength of our enterprise crisis management program, but also exposed some pretty ugly warts. Some leaders believed they had planned for everything, including active threats, bomb scares or fires. But we were not prepared for a Black Swan event. (See chapter 18, "Black Swan or Gray Rhino?")

Security and resilience are services that do not make money for the company. They are an expense that is placed on the Selling, General & Administrative (SG&A) line of a company's income statement. Like similar services, they are typically funded at a minimal or compliance level. The best programs are directly tied to achieving the company's business goals and are funded by the business units who have come to understand security and resilience's necessity to achieve goals.

As a result, when companies set their budgets, including their crisis management strategy, the focus is on what is likely to happen that would disrupt the company's ability to operate, create, and deliver products and/or services. Typically, the planning addresses the top five to ten potential crisis-level disruptions. Pandemics are included in the crisis management resilience plan, well, almost never.

As Dan Sauvageau, a retired *Fortune* 500 CSO observed, "Some businesses and CSOs were completely caught off guard while more astute leaders and organizations had contagious illness groups and plans at the ready. Their plans were informed and strengthened by experiences dealing with epidemics and pandemics much smaller in magnitude. For example, H5N1, H1N1, outbreaks of MMR impacting the workplace, Swine Flu, Ebola and others. Even though none of these compare to the impact Covid-19 has had on humanity and business, having operational plans to deal with smaller issues formed the chassis to build upon and the muscle memory from which to respond more capably and quickly."

To address economic reality and be prepared, organizations create a crisis management committee or group (CMG) that is not uniquely funded. They are not like the fire department who are paid to wait for a fire alarm. These group members have a full-time primary role and function, subject matter expertise, and management skills to support crisis management, but are not singularly dedicated to it. Typical models include the department head leaders as members from Security, Safety, Facilities, Legal, HR, IT, Operations, Finance, Corporate Communications. They have executive oversight from the C-suite and typically report progress, options, and recommendations to that organization.

Dan Sauvageau worked with several companies during the crisis and shared,

> I observed astute security leaders take the opportunity to lead in this crisis, leveraging similar skills used to manage myriad past natural, man-made and political crises. Their ability to think on their feet, build cross functional teams in the face of fear, uncertainty and despair caught the attention of their CEO's. After all, most typical corporate services functions such as such as HR, Legal, Business Leaders do not have the breadth and depth of crisis management as experienced and connected Security and Resilience leaders. I guarantee that long after the pandemic ends the executive leadership will remember who "showed up" for the ultimate "snow day." There is a saying among many first responders that in times of crisis there are those "who make it happen" "watch it happen" and show up late to ask, "what happened?" This was a crisis where companies needed people to "make it happen" because there was no single play book to follow.

Several organizations in the health care and medical industries have chief medical or health officers they rely upon. Most crises are not medical, and having this resource is not typical or typically needed for an effective response to the event. CMGs with medical subject matter expertise expressed significant benefits to their crisis management response, including having the medical/health executive leader chair the CMG. Those without medical or health expertise hired consultant companies, such as International SOS, or fractional chief medical officers to fill this gap.

Dan Sauvageau continued, "Privately contracted risk firms like International SOS, IJET and public agencies such as The International Security Management Association (ISMA), Overseas Security Advisory Committee (OSAC), The Center for Disease Control (CDC), and the World Health Organization (WHO) are very valuable in a health care crisis like COVID-19. But since most CSOs or any other corporate leader for that matter have no expertise in health, epidemiology, virology, it is important to have consultants or contacts who are expert and can explain the science allowing leaders to make informed decisions. This was a crisis that required "out of the box" thinking and leveraging experts with different expertise, such as data science or AI, was important."

The CMG's work includes updating plans to reflect changes, resourcing, holding tabletop exercises, and remaining current with compliance, personnel, and business changes. The CMG also sets approved communication protocols including final decision authority. Historically, this has worked for the foreseeable, but unplanned, disruption.

CMGs are well-oiled machines for the severe, but short-term, discreet business disruption requiring high resilience to detect, respond, and recover from a crisis. And their reactions and training are to go *all in*, dedicating full energy to the crisis at hand. Earthquakes, terror, accidents, fires, power failures, or political unrest are events that are discreet. They happen, and they end. You catch up on your sleep when it is over.

But COVID-19 was not typical. It is the snow day turned snow years.

On March 11, 2020, the World Health Organization (WHO) declared COVID-19 a pandemic. There was no know treatment or vaccine. Global equity markets dropped sharply in March while unemployment rates soared. Uncertainty was the only certainty in the moment.

The pandemic quickly became a complex global crisis that created a cross-domain challenge for organizations and, as an outcome, a power vacuum. There was no clarity on who had the snow day authority as the size and scope of the decisions increased. For example, CMGs were well-set to decide to initiate temperature screening and determine how to facilitate them. But that is not at the same scale as closing down an operating facility. The power vacuum was not the result of negative intent. Rather, it was due to the vastness of the pandemic response decision matrix.

In some organizations, a fear arose between existential risk to the business and health consequences resulting from exposure to the virus. Medical experts may be comfortable with a health-related recommendation to close, but not personally comfortable with the business impact of that decision. And equally, a business leader willing to make the resilience decision to continue operations may not be willing to own the decision's negative health and wellness impact.

As Dan Sauvageau reflected, "Training is essential but the emphasis should be on 'realistic training' that is placed under conditions that mirror a real crisis. Challenges including limited and changing facts, limited and questionable intel sources, 'fog' and uncertainty and emotions come into play in a real crisis. Over the past ten years or so, the speed and volume at which information and misinformation travels needs to be included in training the recommendation and decision processes, as there are both advantages and disadvantages that come with it."

The pandemic was unlike the discreet events crisis management teams plan and train for. At this writing in March 2021, one year since its arrival. January 2021 was the worst recorded month for infections and deaths in the US. Several CSOs commented they began to shift strategy about July 2020 to manage this as a marathon and not a sprint. After months of 24-7 work, they encouraged their teams to take time off and focus on their families and their own health. As one CSO shared:

> I learned more in the past year than at any time during my 35-year career. You come to think that you have seen it all, experienced it all and nothing new will surprise you. But being hit by a Black Swan event that keeps evolving has been, for lack of a better word, an education.

The responses were varied on timing, but not dramatically. Most enterprises learned of the pandemic's rise in Wuhan, China, in January 2020; and by the end of that month, they were fully operating a crisis management response and holding CMG meetings.

As a group, CMGs discussed the implications of the newly identified coronavirus and the impact to the team in broader China as its spread began moving outside of Wuhan. Within weeks to a month, most organizations had expanded the CMG team across Asia. And they realized this may be bigger than they knew based on intelligence from boots on the ground reports. In January 2020, the first case was reported in the United States.

"Our international offices were impacted first and they initially rang the alarm. Perhaps because it started outside the US or perhaps because there was an initial level of complacency in the public, the virus was downplayed. And that resulted in varying levels of alarm," shared one CSO.

Having a mature CMG enabled enterprises to rapidly assemble the appropriate personnel (and support functions) and create a "one company" approach, allowing for rapid decision-making and effective communications. This decision was important to their success because it meant there would be one response to communicate and execute against the pandemic.

Most of the participant enterprises had a preexisting core of personnel (several dozen) within multiple functions that had previously participated in crisis events or their annual training tabletop exercises. Because of the size, scale, and duration of this event and the massive impact it had, these enterprises realized they would need to stand up regional incident management teams and policy advisory groups to speed decision-making and recommendations to the company:

- They expanded the geographic response area as the forecasted spread of the virus became evident.
- They increased their CMG to add subgroups to increase their bench strength and added flexibly to respond to regional needs.
- The subgroups reduced the time to execute their response, including anticipating the need for testing, contact tracing teams, and in some cases forming pod agreements within the organization. They were also well-placed to quickly acquire and distribute PPE and cleaning supplies.
- They increased communications to the board and C-suite, including daily meetings.

COVID-19 was like nothing these enterprises had been through before, but their underlying CMG plans worked. Adjustments were made based on the size and scale; the ebb and flow of spread being both geographically uneven while also global. And they adjusted where the snow day decision lived by stating, "We don't know." Not knowing and not knowing *yet* are very different things. The CMGs functioned by bringing the unknown to the executive committee and asking, "Who owns this decision?" during this new, uncharted crisis response.

"There comes a point in any crisis, as it grows, when you need to face it head on and know who is in charge. You have to look around the table and agree on who is going to lead," stated Dan Sauvageau.

As the virus spread in the US, most enterprises discussed the impact on their employees as core to business resilience, and they decided a virtual environment was most desirable, as much as it was feasible. They shifted all stakeholders who did not have to be on-site to remote locations, mostly to their homes. In most cases, the decision to shift to a virtual work environment was made before knowing exactly how it would be accomplished.

Companies relied, successfully for the most part, on their employees to "figure it out," which most did. The work-from-home shift occurred ahead of their IT departments, who were charged with supporting the shift. Companies relied on their IT departments to support remote workflows with connectivity and access. Once the business was functioning, IT worked to provide information security by adding VPNs and migrating employees from personal to company devices. Schools and universities followed a similar path, facilitating the shift from on-premise to remote learning instruction.

For some companies and employees, working remotely was a normal part of their culture. Software engineers in Silicon Valley or sales representatives covering a regional territory were well versed in the remote work culture. Other enterprises held employees who are wired for structure and routine: Getting up, getting dressed, going to work, and going home. For some, they had neither the remote location nor personal nature to flourish in a less-structured work environment.

For many enterprises, it quickly became clear this was going to take a long time for employees to adapt. Some embraced it and got in front of the change by configuring a home office. Others could not manage the change as well. Most of the enterprises we spoke with responded by creating a new organization or creating resources to help the company and managers work "differently."

The potential impact these changes might have on mental health from isolation and lack of collaboration, including loneliness or depression because they could no longer "go" to work following their established routines, was readily acknowledged. Some organizations relied on their Employee Assistance Program (EAP) for confidential support to help those facing challenges. Others provided different resources. Especially effective was having managers and other leaders directly contact employees, not to discuss business or performance, but to engage them on how they were doing personally.

"In January we expected this to be over by June and we came out of the gate at a full sprint. In April we were not even close to done. And I thought: I am not going to make it. I have to learn how to pace myself. The demands of the first six months of the crisis felt like they were 24/7. I moved from the sprint to the marathon mentality," shared an executive.

Executive leaders saw it as part of their job to stay engaged and reach out more now than ever. They reached out to team members not only to check in on those that tested positive or had other issues, but to help them evolve their thinking. They encouraged their hardworking team members to take some long weekends, explaining this was going to be a grind.

They also focused on being transparent by both acknowledging this was going to go on for a long time while emphasizing that this was a moment in time and would pass. Many encouraged their teams to adopt the "marathon, not a sprint" perspective. The conversations included both a positive look to the future but maintained the current reality. They expressed the positive outlook that there were vaccines and vaccinations on their way. But were also honest about the short-term workload that each day would greet them with a full, new work set. Mostly, they shared empathy with the situation, encouraged them to seek any needed support, and focused on proactive, open lines of communication.

Underlying the CMG's decision-making process was a strong reliance on intelligence sources and data analysis. Enterprises increased their radar by gathering and analyzing information from the CDC, Johns Hopkins, ISMA, ASIS CSO Center for Excellence, the Association of Chief Medical Officers, and especially their rolodexes. From prior military, law enforcement, and private sector experience, peer-to-peer sharing was critically valuable.

Enterprises also faced both a compliance requirement and a health resource with the local health departments where they operated. Compliance with social distancing, PPE, remote work for nonessential roles, testing, and reporting cases to the (typically) county required new workflows. But it also gave guidance on best practices to reduce spread and improve resilience.

They also created internal tools to support the response. Many relied on apps that allowed employees to enter self-diagnostic information for immediate instruction and broad analysis.

An executive outlined their program: "We created a tool that tracked positive tests and close contacts by employees. Another tool allowed us to identify and assign a phased return-to-work date for every employee. And we have developed a tool based on CDC guidance that will help us prioritize individuals within our work force that might be eligible to be vaccinated based on the assigned status of critical infrastructure with Phase 1B."

But there were areas where their investment in security technology came up short for managing access to facilities and ensuring safety.

"Most companies would have been better prepared if they had more robust virtual platforms and systems to allow GSOC operators to work remotely in a more resourced manner. They would have benefitted from robust analytics on access controls and video systems including people detection and counting," summarized Dan Sauvageau.

Critical to success was effectively overcommunicating the response plan, progress, changes, and providing information on resources from answering questions to requesting medical support. Many enterprises developed a coronavirus "hotline" and a dedicated COVID-19 website to facilitate communications in a configured and controlled manner with employees.

This investment in the core crisis management plan, communications, was at the ready; and it was paying dividends when applied to COVID-19 information for a dynamically changed work force. In addition to numerous COVID-19 communications being released through websites and social media, enterprises held subteam calls with CMG leaders and subject matter experts to address regional concerns.

After PPE equipment was acquired and rules were put in place, compliance became a significant issue. The new work included creating and ensuring safe environments with a high level of discipline and compliance. All organizations interviewed followed CDC guidelines. Many exceeded recommendations by having longer quarantine periods in place. Outside the US, some countries had more aggressive rules requiring US-based enterprises to meet those requirements where they did business. Most enterprises made the decision to require PPE be worn, treating it like any other piece of safety gear, such as hard hats.

A global CSO shared, "We made the decision that whether an employee was at one of our facilities or at a customer site, our safety requirements were the rule. If the company they were working at did not require PPE, they were still required to follow our policy. And we terminated some employees for violating the policy."

Companies again overcommunicated the importance of following these new rules, the reasons for them, and the processes to be compliant. Educating the benefits behind the PPE requirements of mask wearing, social distancing, and washing hands paid dividends by creating understanding and achieving the required behavior. PPE compliance became an added task for the security and safety teams to remind employees to wear masks and maintain distance.

Many organizations, not all, extended the communications to other stakeholders, including customers, supply chain partners, and (student) parents by sharing what they were doing and updating their progress on battling the virus, tracking cases, and supporting employee safety.

During the second quarter of 2020, US infection and death rates declined. And some organizations moved to reopen, in hindsight, too soon. The spread was trending down, and as one leader shared, "We got lulled into a false sense of security as the numbers dipped in May, because in early June the numbers took off as infections surged to three or four times what they had been. We responded by scaling up the hotlines and testing facilities."

Six months into the COVID-19 crisis management response, the short burst of optimism was quickly shattered.

Through all of this crisis, budgets, business, and potential downsizing was never far from mind. Revenue was low, and the crisis management spend high. Would the company make it? Security teams were working tirelessly to keep the company as operational, safe, and secure as possible. Would they be recognized and rewarded? Or simply met with a layoff?

The onset of a crisis is not the time for any department, including security, to start defending its value. And it is too early to understand the long-term impact of the pandemic on the US economy, individual businesses, and how organizational structures will be changed in a new, uncertain normal.

As one security leader summarized, "I think the pandemic once again shined the light of the value of the CSO role and that of a strong security organization. Our skill set within crisis management have been the foundational building blocks of a successful response. The key to everything was having top—down buy-in. And it was not our first crisis, so leadership had experience with and confidence in the CMG. That drove our ability to act and respond quickly to the crisis."

The next wave of work for security and resilience teams will be supporting the vaccination process, decisioning on vaccination policy, and compliance methods related to business travel and service providers who enter their premises. Most complex will be managing the risks created by the new work-from-home culture.

Indeed, this was a different type of crisis. CEOs and boards of directors have been forced to take crisis management and resilience seriously and revisit planning and budgeting. The leaders who were trusted and respected during their body of work were the go-to executives to manage the crisis.

Many tirelessly put their well-thought-through plans to work and guided their enterprises through the crisis. But no plan was perfect, and every leader was sincere in their appraisal that constant flexibility and learning during the crisis provided the path to a successful outcome.

CHAPTER 18

STRATEGIC PLANNING: BLACK SWAN OR GRAY RHINO?

> *Before the discovery of Australia, people in the Old World were convinced that all swans were white, an unassailable belief as it seemed completely confirmed by empirical evidence.*

> —*The Black Swan*, Nassim Nicholas Taleb

Taleb is a Lebanese-American essayist, scholar, mathematical statistician, and former option trader and risk analyst, whose work concerns problems of randomness, probability, and uncertainty. As a young man, it was unimaginable that Lebanon's civil war would break out, and rational, intelligent, and tolerant people would fight for fifteen years and kill over ninety thousand people. His studies and work in financial markets and as an essayist were built from his experiences during his youth.

He places black swans as the catalyst for many events in the world, from religions to his personal life (*The Black Swan: The Impact of the Highly Improbable* by Nassim Nicholas Taleb [goodreads.com]).

Nick Hare wrote,

> *As used by Taleb, a "black swan" is a failure of imagination in which, instead of a high-impact hypothesis or outcome being appraised and discounted, it is simply not considered*

at all. Taleb's story is that until black swans were actually discovered, it was simply assumed that they did not exist. (www.alephinsights.com)

There has been significant discussion whether COVID-19 was a Black Swan event. There is a compelling counterargument that COVID-19 was the opposite of a Black Swan, but rather a Gray Rhino event. And perhaps most intriguing is that the person who coined the phrase and wrote *The Black Swan* (2007), Taleb himself, does not believe COVID-19 was a Black Swan event.

Technically, it was widely known that pandemics had happened before. That they did, indeed, exist. And there was discussion in medical circles and more generally led by interviews in mass media with Bill Gates that a major, foreseeable disruption was probable, and it would be a pandemic.

Thus, it was not that societies, governments, and businesses and institutions did not believe pandemics existed. But rather, that the risk of a pandemic occurring did not exist or the possibility was so minute it did not deserve serious attention and defense preparedness. Thinking toward earthquakes in San Francisco is similar.

Comparatively, a gray rhino is a metaphor coined by risk expert Michele Wucker in her book *The Gray Rhino: How to Recognize and Act on the Obvious Dangers We Ignore* (April 2016) to describe "highly obvious, highly probable, but still neglected" dangers, as opposed to unforeseeable or highly improbable risks—the kind in the black swan metaphor.

In her book, Ms. Wucker explains the critical importance of understanding the risk you are facing, and it directly impacts crisis management strategy and planning:

> *It matters immensely that decision-makers view risks as gray rhinos instead of obsess in vain about black swans, because we can see gray rhinos in front of us, but black swans by definition only appear in the rearview window. That means we have a chance to do something about gray rhinos. And, in fact, most so-called black swans happen because people ignored the gray rhinos.*

Risks are often identified as having the potential to happen but are not mitigated because the risk of occurrence is believed low enough that the cost to mitigate against them is considered too expensive, leaving a known vulnerability in place.

As Jack Briggs noted in his interview, "In my work, I learned to not get stuck thinking only about the most dangerous things that could happen. If I let myself think, "It could happen" my mind would run away to the absolute worst thing it could come up with. Most of those things, the most dangerous ones, turn out to be existential to the organization with little I could do to fix them. Instead, I spent more time addressing what was most likely to happen just short of existential. Those are the most likely large things, the really damaging events. In business resilience and disaster management planning, resilience against small things is typically well planned and responded to. Those are the most likely small things and organizations have operational flows and teams in place who can handle the situation within their unit and recover."

As an example, Super Storm Sandy was named a Black Swan by the National Geographic (blog.nationalgeographic.com) but was actually a Gray Rhino based on changing weather patterns. The changing weather threats to the New York City area led to discussions and rejections for investing to protect the city.

In fact, it was so well-known that the Museum of Modern Art hosted an exhibit titled Rising Currents in 2010, over two years before Superstorm Sandy occurred:

RISING CURRENTS: PROJECTS FOR NEW YORK'S WATERFRONT PROPOSES

INFRASTRUCTURE SOLUTIONS FOR THE EFFECTS OF CLIMATE CHANGE

MoMA Exhibition Showcases Sustainable Proposals by Teams of NYC Architects

Rising Currents: Projects for New York's Waterfront

March 24–October 11, 2010

The Robert Menschel Architecture and Design Gallery, third floor

NEW YORK, March 4, 2010—Rising Currents: Projects for New York's Waterfront, a major initiative organized by The Museum of Modern Art and P.S.1 Contemporary Art Center to propose solutions for the effects of climate change on New York's waterfronts, culminates in an exhibition at The Museum of Modern Art from March 24 through October 11, 2010. The exhibition presents architectural proposals that emphasize adaptive "soft" infrastructure solutions for New York and New Jersey's Upper Bay to make New York City and surrounding areas more resilient in responding to rising sea levels and more frequent storm surges. (www.moma.org, press release)

Ron Scherer wrote "How Will New York Keep Out a Rising Sea? Many Options, Little Consensus" (November 15, 2012, www.abcnews.go.com).

The costs to protect the city were high and widely varied from $2 to $15 billion. Post Sandy, New York governor Andrew Cuomo estimated the direct costs to the state at $42 billion (not including indirect costs to businesses, transportation systems, and reduced tax receipts). The total cost of the storm was $70 billion in 2012.

The nuance in these definitions is that a Gray Rhino, such as climate change, makes Super Storm Sandy a predictable event. And that event is named a Black Swan when it does occur. COVID-19 fits this shift that the pandemic was both predicted and predictable, but still considered a Black Swan when it actually arrived.

The Wisdom Project's Wisdom Letter #28, "Of Black Swans and Grey Rhinos," (The Wisdom Project [www.wisdomproject.substack.com]) points out that Gray Rhinos are somewhat the opposite of a Black Swan. Climate Change is an often-used example of a Gray Rhino that we are aware of, see its impact, and can do something to defend against it. However, not addressing it may lead to an irreversible Black Swan event. The pandemic is viewed in the same way. Further, a Gray Rhino can become a Black Swan event. Flu pandemics are not unknown and have been discussed as either likely or inevitable. Thus, a Gray Rhino that could have been better prepared and defended against before it changed to a Black Swan.

Logically (or illogically), if either climate change, pandemics, or earthquakes are not believed to "exist," then their arrival or discovery can only be defined as a Black Swan.

In the Axios article "Coronavirus and Climate Change Are Obvious Risks We Ignore" (www.axios.com), author Amy Harder points out the differences between the two:

> *While coronavirus and climate change are both gray rhino risks, their differences explain why the world—and stocks and oil prices—are suddenly in tailspins.*

It was responded to as both. The US Government began developing vaccines for severe acute respiratory syndrome (SARS) in 2003, which sped the development of COVID-19 vaccines in 2020 (https://jbiomedsci. biomedcentral.com/articles/10.1186/s12929–020–00695–2). The vaccine development was the result of treating the risk of a pandemic outbreak as a Gray Rhino. But the safety precautions such as manufacturing masks or hand sanitizers that could be widely distributed was a Black Swan response to COVID-19. It is interesting that the two responses from the same crisis management task force at the White House happened simultaneously.

For crisis management planning, differentiating between these two definitions is important because the strategy, preparation, and training need to be different. But as Wucker points out, viewing risk through the lens of a Gray Rhino event based on predictable metrics built from real world data keeps threats in front of you. You can do something about a Gray Rhino in your planning, risk presentations to the board, and craft cost/benefit scenarios to ensure different resilience outcomes.

CHAPTER 19

TECHNOLOGY MATTERS

*In 1963 David Ogilvy, the father of Madison Avenue and author of a classic business book, "Confessions of an Advertising Man," wrote: "An advertisement is like a radar sweep, constantly hunting new prospects as they come into the market. Get good radar, and keep it sweeping." Half a century later advertisers are at last taking him at his word. Behavioural profiling has gone viral across the internet, enabling firms to reach users with specific messages based on their location, interests, browsing history and demographic group. Ads can now follow users from site to site: a customer who looks online for flights to Frankfurt will be inundated with German holiday offers. Conversant, a digital-marketing firm uses an algorithm to deliver around 800,000 variations of an ad to its big clients' prospective customers to make it as irresistible as possible. Kraft, a food company, monitors online opinions on its brands in an office which it calls "the looking glass." (**The Economist, Little Brother, September 2014**)*

We may not realize how much marketing's mission is intertwined with security's. Perhaps a digital marketing conference would be as valuable to those leading resilience and security as attending a security industry event because the era of collecting, analyzing, and synthesizing data to recognize risks and identify threats through a predictive posture has arrived. Technology that brings intelligence into an organization about threats or opportunities improves predictability and allows focusing resources. Marketing focuses on the person most likely to buy. Security focuses on the threats most likely to occur.

The Predictive Revolution (2014) chronicled the beginning of the shift in risk and security strategy and investments to refocus security strategy toward business resilience.

From Reactive to Predictive

The Reactive Era defines most of physical security's strategy and history. Similar to the TV show "Law and Order" where each episode begins by discovering a dead body, reactive security programs wait for the phone to ring or an alarm to sound. Security responds to an incident that has happened, initiates a report and if indicated, a follow-up investigation.

Manned officer patrols may come upon a crime in progress or provide a visible deterrent. But the crime statistics prove otherwise. Historically, a reactive posture was the standard procedure.

But 9/11 changed the American public's awareness and understanding of not proactively preparing against. The cost of a reactive security posture went far beyond just economic disruption to an existential capacity for businesses and the economy to function. The 9/12 impact shifted Duty of Care toward preventing disruptive events enabling enterprises to be resilient and continue to successfully function. Building resilience through a predictive posture to withstand disruptions including active shooters, political unrest, theft, terror or pandemic required a shift in leadership and an investment in technology, people and processes. Supporting business resilience became central to security's mission, strategy and budget approval.

The perceived cost of risk increased in both the public's awareness and insurer's actuary tables (Note: The insurance industry paid out $32 billion to 9/11 specific claims leading to the Terrorism Risk Insurance Act in the United States being passed. The legislation shared losses between the federal government and the insurance industry enabling insurers to include terrorism insurance at an affordable premium level.) (^https://

www.investopedia.com/ask/answers/050115/what-impact-have-terrorist-attacks-had-insurance-industry.asp)

Spending on security and safety changed from a hidden to a visible component of the college tour, prospective employee visits, sporting and entertainment event venues and business-to-business sales presentations.

These dynamic shifts also caused the familiar "guns, guards and gates" security mantra to wane. Enterprises sought business executives to lead the risk and security discipline and the Chief Security Officer role matured in seniority and selection with business-minded leaders with risk and security subject matter expertise heavily recruited. And security became big business.

9/11 drove significant venture investment for security technologies to screen airport passengers, air and sea cargo and defend border crossings while enabling commerce. For enterprises, the digitizing of security technology would begin the slow transition onto the corporate network and IT management. Digitizing also reduced the total cost of ownership for security technology systems and the ability to move and share information. That began the move to digital or IP solutions and brought both IT into the buying process and moved physical security devices onto the corporate network.

To achieve this goal, the budget shifted from spending most security budget on manual processes to investing in technologies that deliver business value and performance as both force multipliers and information sensors. Eliminating the manned task of checking IDs or recognizing people through repetition was replaced with automation. Locked doors that could be opened with a valid ID badge held against an access control reader became the new normal. Security cameras surveilled the transaction. The cost was lower and the accuracy higher; as an individual might not be aware a known person had been fired the day before; but the ID system would be changed to lock out the badge from granting access.

Being Proactive was the big step forward, with being predictable the big payoff. The Predictive Era emerged by identifying foreseeable risks. Security organizations could take steps to eliminate vulnerabilities against known threats. Predictive Security aimed technology and intelligence analysis toward preventing events from occurring and better allocating resources toward a more effective response.

Like marketers who leverage technology to gather information and build intelligence to predict future buying behavior; physical, cyber and intelligence security operations centers (SOCs) work to predict and prevent events that will negatively impact business continuity, infrastructure and stakeholders.

The Predictive posture maximizes enterprise resilience. It is also the business strategy for security programs that is gaining budget approval. Increasingly, it is the IT department and technology company vendors that are delivering predictive solutions, displacing the traditional physical security decision-making authority for managers set in a reactive posture.

Resilience

Threats and vulnerabilities are not the same thing. There is a risk your car will be stolen in the United States, as 209 are each day. If you leave your car unlocked with the key in it, you have a vulnerability. If a car thief, the threat, attempts to steal your car, the risk will materialize, and your car will be stolen. Threats can be mitigated by identifying and eliminating vulnerabilities, in this case locking the car and taking your key with you. It mitigates the risk against the threat (car thief) finding a vulnerability. Vulnerabilities do not always result in an incident. If the car thief does not target your unlocked car, then the threat does not materialize against the vulnerability. Your car is not stolen, but the risk remains.

But how *resilient* are you without a car? What is the time investment to file a police report, settle an insurance claim, shop and buy a replacement? What was the convenience cost to get to the police station? Visit car dealerships? Commuting to work, perhaps getting children to school and other tasks? What was the total cost of being reactive?

Such is life in the United States. As a society, we live with risk in our everyday lives. Otherwise, it would be impossible to function in today's economy, society, or culture. To reduce risk, we allocate limited resources for security, emergency management, law enforcement, fire and medical emergency response, for example, against known threats.

> *We plan for the worst case, but budget for the best.* (Bob Hayes, managing director, Security Executive Council)

Acquiring, synthesizing, and analyzing data build models that identify the risks against stakeholders, infrastructure, and property. And that data generates "money ball" like intelligence that directs accurate risk management program decisions. But Americans, as a society, do not spend against known threats equal to their risk of happening.

The following examples show how our resilience investment decisions have economic cost and impact, as well as are more preventable through a predictive than a reactive posture.

Governments, insurance companies, automobile manufacturers work to educate drivers on safe practices, including to not text, to not drink and drive, to wear seat belts, and to obey speed limits. Yet, on average, 38 thousand die in automobile accidents, and 4.4 million are injured annually in the United States. The CDC states:

> *About 38,000 people are killed in motor vehicle traffic crashes each year in the United States.[1] Traffic crash deaths resulted in $55 billion in medical and work loss costs in addition to the immeasurable burden on the victims' families and friends in 2018.* (State-Specific Costs of Motor Vehicle Crash Deaths | Motor Vehicle Safety | CDC Injury Center)

And we have to eat. Annually, over 48 million people become ill from foodborne illness, of which 180 thousand are hospitalized and 3 thousand die. For many, speed and convenience outweigh the known risks. The USDA places the annual cost of foodborne illness at $16 billion.

The United States has an ongoing debate on gun safety and legislation to restrict gun ownership and access. About 43 thousand died from gunshot wounds in 2020, including 23 thousand self-inflicted deaths, according to the CDC. The House Joint Economic Committee Report published in 2019 estimated gun violence cost in the United States at $229 billion per year.

About twenty die each year from parachute jumping accidents. You may think parachute jumping is dangerous, but you are twenty-three times more likely to die during a car ride than a parachute jump.

As a society, company, institution, political organization, or government agency, choices are made to spend limited dollars against specific risks. Choices are made to not spend, also, but understand the potential of a higher cost when a threat materializes into a crisis.

Benjamin Franklin's famous idiom, "An ounce of prevention is worth a pound of cure," has been shared for over three hundred years. We know it. But we do not adhere to it. The above statistics are presented to exemplify daily cost/benefit decisions when evaluating risks. They present the "ounce of prevention" in hindsight.

No government, enterprise, school, or parent can keep everyone safe from everything. Risk is all around our world, and we have learned to accept it, reduce it, and recover from its negative, often devastating impact. But it is proven that complacency will not bode well for crisis resilience over time.

But by shifting spending from the "security theater" approach of having guards and gates spread evenly regardless of risk metrics is a failed approach. Gathering intelligence, identifying risks, and creating a predictive posture against known threats builds business resilience that is core to the enterprise's mission.

There Is Always a Crisis

Effective crisis management requires the speed and accuracy of information collection, analysis, synthesis, and action.

"The unexpected doesn't wait for your team to be ready," shared Michael Sher, the president and founder of GroupDoLists. He is an expert and leader in the emergency and incident management markets.

Crises come unexpectedly and frequently. Enterprises are challenged and disrupted constantly by events that are both discrete and localized. They start, are devastating, but they tend to stop relatively soon after they start. And they are usually isolated to disrupting a subset of operations. Unlike the COVID-19 pandemic, most do not have the long-lasting and devastating global impact to health, life, economy, activity, and culture.

During the pandemic, there were many threats that became crises while enterprises worked to manage through the pandemic.

The bad guys were not standing still. Their activity and motivation is constant. When one penetration effort fails, they try others to gain physical and logical system access.

Criminal actors are not always external. Stakeholders including customers, students, and employees are potential threats to an enterprise's assets, people, and infrastructure.

Weather-, natural disaster-, and human error–created crises are far less subjective. They just happen as the culmination of a Gray Rhino or as an outright Black Swan. COVID-19 arrived in this manner. And Dr.

Jean-Jacques Muyembe Tamfum, the doctor who discovered Ebola, warns that the next deadly "disease X is set to hit mankind," but the when is not yet known (*Daily Mail*).

During COVID-19, the crisis management leaders we interviewed pointed out that there are always crises; and during the pandemic, they faced additional ones. Theft was ongoing, and empty facilities became hot targets. Fires in the western United States required employee evacuations as well as shifting operations to other geographies. The SolarWinds cybersecurity breach impacted over eighteen thousand customers, including the US Government. While the number of transportation accidents was reduced due to the work-from-home shift, there were still vehicle accidents and injuries.

Enterprise security teams are constantly on point to identify, prevent, or respond to acts of terrorism, kidnapping and ransom, fraud, active shooters, ransomware, political unrest, protests, labor disputes, extreme weather, natural disasters, power supply failures, supply chain disruptions, and more. Battling the onslaught of threats without a powerful technology and intelligence system for critical event management would be impossible. It is nearly so with one.

The advent of a critical event is not the time to search for the outdated, printed, business resilience binder or find information sources to inform on what is happening. Trying to initiate a crisis management program as the crisis unfolds is too late for achieving a resilient outcome.

Being informed, aware, and prepared requires a glimpse into the future and a whole lot of the present. And those profiled in *Snow Day* are using predictive technology solutions with skilled analysts and operators to create a predictive risk posture, increase resilience, and align their mission and budget with the enterprise's business (and in some cases existential) goals.

Different technology solutions deliver a transformative approach to managing security and risk information faster and smarter. These investments are directed at gathering and synthesizing data for accurate situational awareness and identifying the best options and recommendations for crisis management.

Brian Solis defines digital transformation "as the realignment of, or new investment in, technology, business models, and processes to drive new value for customers and employees and more effectively compete in an ever-changing digital economy" (briansolis.com). The impact on our lives is profound.

Enterprises should constantly reevaluate their risk and resilience programs from where they live in the organization—who leads the team, how budgets are created, and mostly how to digitize crisis management for better resilience and life safety.

The Predictive Revolution

Hand a smart phone to an eleven-year-old, and within moments, you will be speaking to the smartest person in the world. Technology is changing life, daily. But many enterprises still have their business resilience plans printed, in a binder, and out of date.

Smart phones and wireless networks allow us to stay connected and communicate in most geographic locations, freeing us from wired devices and fixed locations. Business information, entertainment, contacts, and messages can be accessed anytime from anywhere because of cloud computing. Having access to the most current information from virtually anywhere for business documents, calendar changes, and personal communications and media consumption brings efficiency while eliminating inconvenience and errors.

Big data examines and finds the tight range of normal. And when an anomaly occurs, that data point is noticed and reported. For example, Google Maps collects the movement of many smart phones from its app, and when all those phones slow down, the road on your phone's map turns yellow. And if the phones all stop, the road on your phone map turns red. The analytics and recommendations engine predicts traffic delays and presents better options to reduce drive time.

At distribution centers, robots are assembling customer orders with complete accuracy, greater speed, and reduced human labor. The value of an accurate order increases customer value, as do lower prices. Customer-facing software integrated to the order-processing system assures the customer that their ordered products are available, ready to be shipped, are shipped, and when they will be delivered. The entire transaction may take less than four hours.

Leveraging new technologies to be predictive and support enterprise goals and ensure resilience is how leading CSOs are growing their responsibilities, budgets, and brand in their organizations. They are proactively reducing manual tasks with automation.

Time is Money. Downtime is Not

Many crises, especially COVID-19, have place tremendous pressure on crisis management teams to achieve resilience. And that demands a holistic view and predictive posture tied to business success.

What are risk and resilience leaders changing? Their focus has shifted from a security-only mindset to a risk management and resilience mindset—that includes security. This broadens the role, business contribution, and resources to do the job. As the narratives in *Snow Day* document, investing in the people and technologies to create and maintain a Predictive Posture improves resilience for the organization's revenue and operations. This approach has measurable results that are winning the C-suite's confidence and support.

Organizations have every opportunity for reinvention by leveraging the digital transformation tools that are happening all around them to create truly valuable and effective programs. The ability to gather data, analyze it, and synthesize it into actionable information that predicts threats, identifies vulnerabilities, and reduces risk, is literally at their fingertips.

Powerful technologies enable these successful outcomes and are changing our world: cloud, big data, robotics, and artificial intelligence / machine learning create the Internet of Things (IoT) foundation; combined with human logic, these empower massive economic and operational performance when applied to crisis management and resilience. They create predictive analytics through information collection, analysis, and operational intelligence. Organizations that are embracing the Predictive Revolution will realize a dramatic increase in the economic value added for their enterprises and stakeholders.

Critical Event Management (CEM)

Critical Event Management is a team sport. Money is invested in CEM programs for one reason, to keep the business and its people safe and operational. Its sole purpose is to prevent, reduce, or recover from a disruptive event. The return on investment is measured in resilience.

Building a holistic CEM requires these key elements:

- Buy in and participation from the CEO.

The CEO is the economic decision-maker and policy leader for risk management and resilience. They have to be aligned with the downside economic and brand risk from a potential crisis and buy off on the value of having a predictive posture to best prevent loss. Without the CEO's support, it is not likely the organization will move past a reactive posture. Having this support is economically, operationally, and culturally vital to sustainability. I wrote in a September 2007 article about Cisco's commitment to resilience and life safety, *"While security has always been a part of the company, it has become part of the culture on a personal level. John Chambers, CEO, participates in crisis management drills."* And that participation, that leadership, set the culture and buy-in among employees to participate and understand critical event management procedures.

- A commitment to digitizing the process.

There are many new technologies and solutions available for CEM. From bringing specific tools into your organization to patch a specific need to "going large" with an enterprise-wide provider—covering policy, people, and technology resources—digitizing CEM is step 1 for success.

The bad news is that you have so many choices; understanding exactly who does what and who integrates with whom can be time-consuming and challenging to process. Setting a committee to research, understand, and match solutions to the strategic CEM plan is the critical second step.

- Understanding that the business unit heads are the internal customers.

The CEM should be built with business unit leadership as the target customer. They are buying business resilience so they can run the business and do their jobs.

They are relying on the operational leaders in IT, Physical Security, Information Security, HR, Legal, Finance, Corporate Communications, and Facilities deliver operational uptime. The group is the core of the enterprise Crisis Management Team (CMT) and partners across disciplines to strategize, plan, train, test, and improve.

A vital part of their work is to build effective communications that cover the following:

1. Communicate what is known.
2. Detail what actions you are taking to address the event and its disruptions.
3. Document that the CEM plan is working through stakeholder feedback.

- Dedicated "volunteers" who have full-time jobs AND are key SMEs for the Critical Event Team.

The narratives in *Snow Day* point to a common theme: that the Crisis Management Team is not staffed with full-time, underutilized employees awaiting a critical event to arise. Quite the opposite, leaders in the company with specialized interest or expertise join the teams and prepare to respond when required.

Crisis management expertise to manage technology in the security operations center (SOC) is required. But that will not be the only trained skill an operator has. They will be skilled at many daily tasks while also prepared to support emergency and crisis events and participate as a core member of the CMT.

Perhaps most underrated is their prior experience working in emergency situations and crisis conditions. Having expertise and calm during an emergency is among the most valuable contributions a crisis team member can make.

- Identify who has snow day authority so that the CMT can present the current situation, options, and a recommendation to best mitigate the crisis. The CMT leader should be communicating with the snow day authority when necessary that a decision needs to be made.

Creating a holistic, end-to-end strategy for crisis event management is not a new or impossible goal, and there are many consultancy and technology companies specializing in helping businesses model, build, and automate their programs.

Framing the CEM with foundational components lay the building blocks for policy, technology, people, and snow day decisions:

Intelligence gathering resources that leverage AI and automation to gather and sift through risk data and push actionable information to analysts for the fastest response are the top of the process funnel. Assessing and organizing your sources of information based on asset location, risk types, asset types, fixed or mobile, and which analysts should manage them prepares the CMT for faster analysis to provide actionable information.

Automated workflows that present approved standard operating procedures, communications, and action plans to CET member devices, regardless of location, speed, teamwork, and better outcomes. Reducing the time to identify and respond to events is most critical for life safety.

Correlating risks with assets to understand if a potential or actual threat will impact an asset or person. Through identifying, locating, and tracking people, critical assets, supply chain, and mobile assets such as vehicles places the CMT in a strong position to manage an event. This also allows interdependencies to be built among assets, showing how one becoming unavailable will impact response and resilience of the others.

Informed decisions built on metrics to ensure the system is getting the right information to the right person at the right time to make the right decision. By analyzing the exposure to the enterprise's assets, people, and processes, the CMT can focus on what is most probable.

Imad Mouline is the chief technology officer for Everbridge and author of *9 Steps to Critical Event Management Improvement*, which addresses the business plan thinking from defining what actually is a critical event for your specific business through assessing the risks and related information sources to be aware of and alerted to those risks materializing.

With over 5,600 customers, Everbridge is the market leader in the CEM space and had hyper growth during the COVID-19 crisis. In a CNBC interview (December 28, 2020), David Meredith, CEO, shared that "Everbridge protects business from disruption and mitigates the effects of critical events." He positioned the pandemic as a wake-up call for CEOs, boards of directors, and government officials to be prepared for events that can happen in the future.

The nine steps mirror Jack Briggs's crisis management strategy and structure he created, including key tie-ins to technology for coordinating data sources and generating information analytics. This includes building the capability to have a (enterprise-wide) common operating picture and automating workflows.

Perhaps the most important step is number 9, Analyzing Performance. As no plan is ever perfect, training, tabletop exercises, and continuously asking "what has changed" and "what can we do better" improves performance, sharpens roles and crisis management outcomes.

Among the experts and leaders in critical event management is Michael Sher, founder and CEO of Groupdolists (Response Reinvented), who lent his expertise and time to *Snow Day*.

"My passion for critical event management comes from my experience on 9/11." Michael had just moved to New York City as a newlywed and recalled the day as thus: "Certainly, it was a horrific day. And the inability to communicate created a tremendous feeling of vulnerability. The Verizon cell tower was down and I could not reach my wife, who was at work. No one could reach friends, family or loved ones. And that inspired me to make a difference."

Michael was introduced to a business executive who had built a notification system to reach and recall nurses for their work shifts. They leveraged that technology for the post–9/11 need to enable larger voice blasts, response and tracking applications. A few months later, SendWordNow had Bank of New York, Bloomberg, and Disney as name customers.

> It was a purpose driven company with a ton of energy and mindset to help organizations and people communicate through a fast and reliable technology that could reach hundreds of thousands of people in a targeted manner, simultaneously.

SendWordNow was neither the first nor the only company in this space. "We had many competitors, probably 45 or more. 9/11 spawned the cloud-based mass notification industry which has gone through steady consolidation over the past 20-years. Dialogic Communications Corporation in Franklin, Tennessee was the de facto standard. They were the first premise-based system. 3N, the National Notification Network, interestingly became Everbridge. And SendWordNow was acquired by the investment firm Veritas in 2017. They also acquired MIR3, Code Red and One Call Now."

The consolidation in mass notification companies has been followed by a boom in new technologies and companies entering the critical event management market. "Buyers face a lot of FUD (fear, uncertainty and doubt) in making decisions and selecting solutions to make the enterprise resilient."

Michael quickly lists off a few:

- Business continuity planning
- Traveler tracking
- Mass notification systems
- Crisis management communications
- Risk intelligence
- Threat intelligence (which is all hazards risk intelligence plus human analysts)

> There is consolidation, such as Everbridge buying NC4 the threat intelligence company. But there are 6 to 8 new threat intelligence companies in the space now. I feel sorry for the buyer because there are so many puzzle pieces to assemble now and it's often difficult to tell one from another.

> And interestingly, we are witnessing consolidation at the CEM level now. Everbridge has been the pioneer in consolidating product companies into a large enterprise solution. And I think you will see more consolidation with second, third and fourth tier players following in their path to create additional, holistic end-to-end solution providers.

Michael launched his new company, Centrallo Corporation, which powers Groupdolists to help the teams responsible for the safety and security of people and assets better and more tightly manage their responses during unexpected incidents. Groupdolists also focuses on digitizing crisis management plans, making them interactive and accessible on any device. By delivering logical, actionable, and recordable instructions, the solution breaks down the plan into steps that can be acted upon and communicated.

> We take the living, but not breathing plan and activate it into an interactive and actionable format. It gives CMT leaders a more organized and fluid view of the situation getting them closer to the critical decisions that best protect life safety.

The biggest changes in this market are Artificial Intelligence (AI) and automation. AI is making decisions for you. And automation is managing the intelligence that comes across your SOC operators desk. For example, if there is an earthquake in an area the AI and automation assesses if you have assets there and if the set Richter threshold is exceeded—that triggers action. The assets, people and other stakeholders in that area will be alerted through messaging communications. CMTs are alerted and assembled and the process is documented *before* any human interaction.

As an example of technology's import for CEM, a Washington, DC, government agency near the US Capitol was impacted by the January 6, 2021, riot ("How News Media Is Describing the Incident at the US Capitol" [visualcapitalist.com]). Groupdolists was utilized to ensure every stakeholder did what they needed to do across the greater region.

It was eye opening to have moved a manual, paper driven process to an automation platform, see that on one sheet of music and have it work as expected. Incident management, communications and the audit trail all worked flawlessly in real time through automated workflows. This is where I think the CEM market is going.

Counter to the Groupdolists' customer experience, the Capitol's crisis management plan resulted in a different outcome. As Forbes contributor Edward Segal wrote after the January 6, 2021, riot, congressional hearings highlighted important crisis management lessons during the testimony of Major General William J. Walker, commanding general of the DC National Guard, who testified "that he did not receive permission from his chain of command at the Pentagon to send forces to the Capitol until three hours and 19 minutes after receiving an urgent call at 1:49 p.m. Jan. 6 from the Capitol Police chief saying a request for Guard backup was imminent," as reported in the *Washington Post*.

Segal points out:

The ability to make and obtain decisions quickly about a crisis—what to do, when to do it, how to do it, where to do it, who will do it, and why to do it—can be the tipping point in how well or poorly companies and organizations respond to a crisis. Time is essential in any crisis. ("Here's the Latest Crisis Management Lesson From the Capitol Riot: Command Chains Matter [forbes.com')

A CMT trained in policy, technology, and people reduces the time to understand the threat, analyze the options, and recommend action, thereby saving time and increasing resilience. New solutions will continue to increase the bandwidth and value of crisis management investments, resulting in higher correlation between a predictive posture and protecting the business mission.

CHAPTER 20

THE LONG WALK TOWARD "NORMAL"

What happens after a crisis? When does the response begin to wane and the recovery begin? When is the recovery completed, if ever? And when does a business close the book on an incident and move forward? These are not easy questions.

There is not one right answer, program, or process that is equal to the task of recovery. Not every person reacts to trauma in the same way, as described in "The Human in Us All" chapter. Nor does the same treatment heal evenly across the affected population.

While some people are able to just "get back to work," "shake it off," or "get over it," there are others for whom the challenges are greater. Dr. Scott Hadland, an addition expert based in Boston, told CNN, "The pandemic has pushed already economically vulnerable Americans into even greater despair" and that "overdose deaths are now surging to record highs" ("The Other Health Crisis the Stimulus Package Will Help," CNN, www.edition. cnn.com).

There is also an uneven contribution and focus on wellness and empathy by varying businesses, institutions, and government programs. Help is offered and available. But that help may not be on target in length or depth. Or it may be rejected by those who need it most.

The variability among the victims, the treatments, and the goals to return to "normal" are an impossible matrix to construct or manage. Every person is unique, and thus each case of trauma and recovery is also unique. Some slip through the cracks to either disappear or return with a vengeance.

Combine this with the understanding and desire to move forward to a new normal in our lives. There have been many traumatic events during the COVID-19 pandemic, including active shooters, fires, natural disasters, massive power failures, vehicular fatalities, other disabling diseases, and financial hardships—to list but a few.

As societies, families as pods, and people as individuals work toward a new normal after any trauma-causing crisis, it is important for businesses and institutions to extend support and care for their stakeholders.

Many cannot "just get over it."

After a critical event, the process of returning to work and a normal schedule and way of life rebuilds certainty and confidence in believing tomorrow will be a step toward normal, without massive disruption, and further remove victims from the critical event and its trauma.

We also live with the economic and societal realities of regaining productivity and achieving (original or restated) goals. That is true in business, school, government, and houses of worship. There is a striving to find normal, and there are bills to pay and lives to live.

As enterprises start to recover from the COVID-19 crisis, concern for their stakeholders' mental health will come into greater focus. There has been a significant investment in protecting people from physical harm, including workplace violence and active shooters; emotional harm including bullying or sexual harassment; and personal harm including substance abuse and suicide. Those investments have built resilience into these organizations that will lead to a stronger and faster recovery.

The return to normal will have its downsides. The United States went nearly a full year without a school shooting. But as schools reopened in 2021 there have been two, both involving fatalities (through March 2021). Increased accidents related to commuting, foodborne illness due to dining out, and other events in daily life that were reduced during the pandemic will statistically increase in frequency. Stakeholders will again require the vigilance and support of their employer's safety and security teams at the pre-COVID-19 activity levels once again.

Enterprise leaders that understand the value of science, a proactive stance against threats, and the importance of human capital as core to business value will invest in supporting their stakeholders' wellness. As the business resilience and physical health impact of the pandemic are mitigated, the focus will shift to mental and emotional support.

Everbridge has published a white paper written by Steve Crimando, the principal and founder of Behavioral Science Applications LLC, an operational risk management consultancy: "Maturing Your Organization's Approach to Work-from-Home: A Focus on Wellness and Productivity," which summarizes the journey we have endured and the link between employee (business) performance and wellness.

First, it recognizes the resilience and crisis management processes that have been implemented:

> *How organizations first reacted was necessary and understandable. On a continuum, we, as humans responding to a threat, tend to move from the "hard" impacts first, then later to the "soft" impacts. Hard impacts include business processes, technologies and the physical structures that house organizations. Soft impacts typically involve people, not processes or technologies. For an organization to effectively fulfill its mission, it must attend to both. For many organizations, attention to remote connectivity, IT security, and virtual meeting platforms, became the initial focal points to enable the workforce to efficiently transition from the employer's facilities to their employee's homes. At some point it became more obvious that public health emergencies are also behavioral health emergencies, and that finding a balance between employee wellness and productivity would be critical to sustaining a work-from-home workforce. Performance and wellness, of course, are intimately linked.*

Noting that the US work-from-home economy accounts for 60 percent of US economic activity and that twice as many employees work from home than traditional workplaces, employers are challenged to provide a heightened and remote duty of care.

Duty of Care means that the employer should take all steps that are reasonably possible to ensure the health, safety, and well-being of their employees. And has typically been applied in an on-premises employment environment. But all employees are due a duty of care, regardless of where they work. And OSHA compliance related to employers providing a safe workplace and ergonomics in a home office are leading to new policies and programs to support remote workers. (Claims of negligence due to work-from-home–related health issues are coming.)

Addressing the issues of mental and physical health, pandemic fatigue, and recognizing employees in distress while remote are the basis for addressing the core issue of productivity. While work-from-home productivity has tracked at higher than pre-pandemic levels, the "this is a marathon, not a sprint" reality will come. And breaks may be built into the workday. IT may just turn off your email or network access for twenty minutes, three times a day, to both protect the employee and the employer.

> *Ninety-four percent of 800 employers surveyed by Mercer, an HR and workplace benefits consulting firm, said that productivity was the same as or higher than it was before the pandemic, even with their employees working remotely.* ("Study Finds Productivity Not Deterred by Shift to Remote Work" [shrm.org])

Employers will want to and need to provide duty of care through communication and support mechanisms, including tools for self-monitoring, buddy care, and team leader/supervisory monitoring. Using the business tools such as videoconferencing or performance reviews for the purpose of ensuring wellness along with productivity may become the new normal for employer-employee relationships.

Recognizing an employee in distress who is not self-aware or not willing to seek help is an important and difficult part of the crisis recovery plan. There are many tools available—from the simple conversation to technology tools. As Mr. Crimando summarizes:

> *Illness or fear of illness, social isolation, economic insecurity, disruption of routine and loss of loved ones are known risk factors for depression and anxiety. Even as vaccines may seem to provide a light at the end of the tunnel for the physical risks of COVID-19, the mental health consequences of the pandemic will likely be more, long lasting, and there is no vaccine for that.*

Restructuring the Mental and Emotional Health Economy

James Lake, MD, writes in "The Mental Health Pandemic Calls for a Strategic Initiative That Emphasizes Integrative Health Care," published October 20, 2020, in *Psychiatric Times*, that

> *even after antivirals and vaccines are developed and contain the spread of the viral pandemic, a mental health pandemic could go on for years, fueled by anticipated long-term economic and social impacts.*

He clearly points out that "history is prologue," and most economies, postcrisis, enter weaker economic cycles from short downturns to prolonged recessions. The negative impact on physical and mental health during the post-9/11 recession and the Great Recession. Dr. Lake notes that

> *the Great Recession of 2007 through 2009 led to a significant increase in rates of cardiovascular disease, cancer, and mental health problems, and worsened the ongoing epidemic of opioid and alcohol abuse.*

And looking forward, he sees similar challenges:

> *Based on history, it is likely that widespread unemployment and food and housing insecurity resulting from economic disruption in the wake of COVID-19 will have similar large-scale impacts on health and mental health, especially among low-income workers and minorities.*

His call to action is that mental health programs deserve the same priority as developing COVID-19 vaccines. But this is a tough call to action in the current health care service structure and cost for delivery. The US Government budget deficit has soared in response to COVID-19. State governments are facing budget deficits as a result of increased COVID-19 spending and reduced tax revenue from its economic impact. Similarly, businesses facing reduced revenue and profit will look to cut employee spending in the short term, not to add new employee benefits. Even if the long-term value and return is foreseeable.

After 9/11, the United States Government created the Department of Homeland Security, including a cabinet-level directorship. Dr. Lake's call for action is similar. He calls for the appointment of a directorship at a cabinet-level to address broad mental health issues including those resulting from the impact of crises. In this case, the COVID-19 pandemic.

> *Successfully implementing an effective mental health care initiative will require shared leadership. It is time for the Department of Health and Human Services, the National Institutes of Mental Health, the American Psychiatric Association, the American Psychological Association, the Institute of Medicine, and experts in mental health care and integrative medicine to join forces and take proactive strategic measures in developing services and resources.*

COVID-19's cost has forced CEOs and boards of directors to take crisis management and resilience seriously by revisiting planning and budgeting. All enterprises would be wise to reconsider how they are delivering mental and emotional support services to their stakeholders not only during this pandemic, but holistically across the horizon of crises they will endure and the new stresses that changing work environments will create. How governments respond and change as an outcome of the pandemic, especially related to the mental and emotional health of its citizens, is unknown.

The economics may have shifted from reducing health care benefits and absorbing the cost of downtime disruption, turnover, and reduced productivity to providing more significant health care benefits to ensure resilience and continuity. Certainly, CEOs and boards of directors have taken interest in the critical event management programs under their responsibility.

CMG teams have a unique opportunity due to the massive disruption and business facility closures caused by the pandemic to gather powerful data from their critical event management pre- and post-cost metrics to reevaluate the economics of crisis management spending against long-term stakeholder wellness and economic value. Holding a Predictive Posture toward individual mental and physical health may now be documented my data as the more profitable path.

The physical and tactical return to company facilities will have logistical challenges, but they are manageable. Perhaps furniture and desks will be partitioned, the process of taking breaks or eating lunch will be reinvented, and a stronger show of custodial activity will be required to build confidence.

The policies for returning employees to the workplace are being determined, including the following:

- Vaccination requirements to return to company facilities.
- Accommodating employees who are not ready or willing to return to a company facility.
- Training employees to function within a new set of behavioral and operational rules.
- Monitoring and addressing employees who do not follow the new rules.

The complex matrix of working through this process will include internal expertise from Legal, HR, Medical, Safety and Security leaders; external policy from local or state health boards and commissions; and in some cases employee unions, associations, or representatives. And it then has to extend to vendors, visitors, customers, etc., to ensure, as best possible, avoiding a resurgence in infections and a renewed health crisis.

For the sports and entertainment business, returning to normal will be a slow process of adding events, increasing attendance, and measuring results. "Gather with A Plan" is the trademark of the Innovation Institute for Fan Experience (i2fx.org), which "works with the world's leading authorities in safety, security and fan experience for a new era focused on health and safety." Executive director Lou Marciani jokes, "Everyone used to want to hide the custodial staff. Now you need to have them highly visible to ensure confidence."

The institute has built an influential international group and peer-to-peer networking to develop a best practices playbook and series of online programs for its members.

Creating confidence that the policies and programs are in place and followed is as important as actually doing them. Marketing and communications are an important part of the process to get people physically back to work, schools, events, and all the other "normal" activities that were pre-pandemic (except blowing out birthday cake candles. That is probably not coming back).

Most of the enterprises and executives interviewed for *Snow Day* were already working toward the return-to-work policies and procedures, including gathering input and communicating decisions. The best practice is focusing on flexibility and empathy during these initial stages.

As Nassim Nicholas Taleb, author of *The Black Swan*, explained to the *New Yorker*:

> *COVID-19 was not a Black Swan event, but was foreseeable. In retrospect, had the U.S. government spent pennies on masks in January 2020 it would have been spared the trillions in stimulus, medical spending and lost tax revenues.*

As COVID-19 vaccinations and herd immunity progress, workers will return to workplaces creating a new critical event to be understood, measured and managed.

APPENDIX

THE 911 COMMISSION REPORT

We now turn to the role of national leadership in the events that morning.

1.3 NATIONAL CRISIS MANAGEMENT

When American 11 struck the World Trade Center at 8:46, no one in the White House or traveling with the President knew that it had been hijacked. While that information circulated within the FAA, we found no evidence that the hijacking was reported to any other agency in Washington before 8:46.[179]

Most federal agencies learned about the crash in New York from CNN.[180] Within the FAA, the administrator, Jane Garvey, and her acting deputy, Monte Belger, had not been told of a confirmed hijacking before they learned from television that a plane had crashed.[181] Others in the agency were aware of it, as we explained earlier in this chapter.

Inside the National Military Command Center, the deputy director of operations and his assistant began notifying senior Pentagon officials of the incident. At about 9:00, the senior NMCC operations officer reached out to the FAA operations center for information. Although the NMCC was advised of the hijacking of American 11, the scrambling of jets was not discussed.[182]

In Sarasota, Florida, the presidential motorcade was arriving at the Emma E. Booker Elementary School, where President Bush was to read to a class and talk about education. White House Chief of Staff Andrew

Card told us he was standing with the President outside the classroom when Senior Advisor to the President Karl Rove first informed them that a small, twin-engine plane had crashed into the World Trade Center. The President's reaction was that the incident must have been caused by pilot error.[183]

At 8:55, before entering the classroom, the President spoke to National Security Advisor Condoleezza Rice, who was at the White House. She recalled first telling the President it was a twin-engine aircraft-and then a commercial aircraft-that had struck the World Trade Center, adding "that's all we know right now, Mr. President."[184]

At the White House, Vice President Dick Cheney had just sat down for a meeting when his assistant told him to turn on his television because a plane had struck the North Tower of the World Trade Center. The Vice President was wondering "how the hell could a plane hit the World Trade Center" when he saw the second aircraft strike the South Tower.[185]

Elsewhere in the White House, a series of 9:00 meetings was about to begin. In the absence of information that the crash was anything other than an accident, the White House staff monitored the news as they went ahead with their regular schedules.[186]

The Agencies Confer

When they learned a second plane had struck the World Trade Center, nearly everyone in the White House told us, they immediately knew it was not an accident. The Secret Service initiated a number of security enhancements around the White House complex. The officials who issued these orders did not know that there were additional hijacked aircraft, or that one such aircraft was en route to Washington. These measures were precautionary steps taken because of the strikes in New York.[187]

The FAA and White House Teleconferences. The FAA, the White House, and the Defense Department each initiated a multiagency teleconference before 9:30. Because none of these teleconferences-at least before 10:00- included the right officials from both the FAA and Defense Department, none succeeded in meaningfully coordinating the military and FAA response to the hijackings.

At about 9:20, security personnel at FAA headquarters set up a hijacking teleconference with several agencies, including the Defense

Department. The NMCC officer who participated told us that the call was monitored only periodically because the information was sporadic, it was of little value, and there were other important tasks. The FAA manager of the teleconference also remembered that the military participated only briefly before the Pentagon was hit. Both individuals agreed that the teleconference played no role in coordinating a response to the attacks of 9/11. Acting Deputy Administrator Belger was frustrated to learn later in the morning that the military had not been on the call.[188]

At the White House, the video teleconference was conducted from the Situation Room by Richard Clarke, a special assistant to the president long involved in counterterrorism. Logs indicate that it began at 9:25 and included the CIA; the FBI; the departments of State, Justice, and Defense; the FAA; and the White House shelter. The FAA and CIA joined at 9:40. The first topic addressed in the White House video teleconference-at about 9:40-was the physical security of the President, the White House, and federal agencies. Immediately thereafter it was reported that a plane had hit the Pentagon. We found no evidence that video teleconference participants had any prior information that American 77 had been hijacked and was heading directly toward Washington. Indeed, it is not clear to us that the video teleconference was fully under way before 9:37, when the Pentagon was struck.[189]

Garvey, Belger, and other senior officials from FAA headquarters participated in this video teleconference at various times. We do not know who from Defense participated, but we know that in the first hour none of the personnel involved in managing the crisis did. And none of the information conveyed in the White House video teleconference, at least in the first hour, was being passed to the NMCC. As one witness recalled,"[It] was almost like there were parallel decision-making processes going on; one was a voice conference orchestrated by the NMCC . . . and then there was the [White House video teleconference].. . . [I]n my mind they were competing venues for command and control and decisionmaking."[190]

At 10:03, the conference received reports of more missing aircraft,"2 possibly 3 aloft," and learned of a combat air patrol over Washington. There was discussion of the need for rules of engagement. Clarke reported that they were asking the President for authority to shoot down aircraft. Confirmation of that authority came at 10:25, but the commands were already being conveyed in more direct contacts with the Pentagon.[191]

The Pentagon Teleconferences. Inside the National Military Command Center, the deputy director for operations immediately thought the second strike was a terrorist attack. The job of the NMCC in such an emergency is to gather the relevant parties and establish the chain of command between the National Command Authority-the president and the secretary of defense- and those who need to carry out their orders.[192]

On the morning of September 11, Secretary Rumsfeld was having breakfast at the Pentagon with a group of members of Congress. He then returned to his office for his daily intelligence briefing. The Secretary was informed of the second strike in New York during the briefing; he resumed the briefing while awaiting more information. After the Pentagon was struck, Secretary Rumsfeld went to the parking lot to assist with rescue efforts.[193]

Inside the NMCC, the deputy director for operations called for an all-purpose "significant event" conference. It began at 9:29, with a brief recap: two aircraft had struck the World Trade Center, there was a confirmed hijacking of American 11, and Otis fighters had been scrambled. The FAA was asked to provide an update, but the line was silent because the FAA had not been added to the call. A minute later, the deputy director stated that it had just been confirmed that American 11 was still airborne and heading toward D.C. He directed the transition to an air threat conference call. NORAD confirmed that American 11 was airborne and heading toward Washington, relaying the erroneous FAA information already mentioned. The call then ended, at about 9:34.[194]

It resumed at 9:37 as an air threat conference call,* which lasted more than eight hours. The President, Vice President, Secretary of Defense, Vice Chairman of the Joint Chiefs of Staff, and Deputy National Security Advisor Stephen Hadley all participated in this teleconference at various times, as did military personnel from the White House underground shelter and the President's military aide on Air Force One.[195]

Operators worked feverishly to include the FAA, but they had equipment problems and difficulty finding secure phone numbers. NORAD asked three times before 10:03 to confirm the presence of the FAA in the teleconference. The FAA representative who finally joined the call at 10:17 had no familiarity with or responsibility for hijackings, no access to decisionmakers, and none of the information available to senior FAA officials.[196]

- *All times given for this conference call are estimates, which we and the Department of Defense believe to be accurate within a 3 minute margin of error.*

We found no evidence that, at this critical time, NORAD's top commanders, in Florida or Cheyenne Mountain, coordinated with their counterparts at FAA headquarters to improve awareness and organize a common response. Lower-level officials improvised-for example, the FAA's Boston Center bypassed the chain of command and directly contacted NEADS after the first hijacking. But the highest-level Defense Department officials relied on the NMCC's air threat conference, in which the FAA did not participate for the first 48 minutes.[197]

At 9:39, the NMCC's deputy director for operations, a military officer, opened the call from the Pentagon, which had just been hit. He began: "An air attack against North America may be in progress. NORAD, what's the situation?" NORAD said it had conflicting reports. Its latest information was "of a possible hijacked aircraft taking off out of JFK en route to Washington D.C." The NMCC reported a crash into the mall side of the Pentagon and requested that the Secretary of Defense be added to the conference.[198]

At 9:44, NORAD briefed the conference on the possible hijacking of Delta 1989. Two minutes later, staff reported that they were still trying to locate Secretary Rumsfeld and Vice Chairman Myers. The Vice Chairman joined the conference shortly before 10:00; the Secretary, shortly before 10:30. The Chairman was out of the country.[199]

At 9:48, a representative from the White House shelter asked if there were any indications of another hijacked aircraft. The deputy director for operations mentioned the Delta flight and concluded that "that would be the fourth possible hijack." At 9:49, the commander of NORAD directed all air sovereignty aircraft to battle stations, fully armed.[200]

At 9:59, an Air Force lieutenant colonel working in the White House Military Office joined the conference and stated he had just talked to Deputy National Security Advisor Stephen Hadley. The White House requested (1) the implementation of continuity of government measures, (2) fighter escorts for Air Force One, and (3) a fighter combat air patrol over Washington, D.C.[201]

By 10:03, when United 93 crashed in Pennsylvania, there had been no mention of its hijacking and the FAA had not yet been added to the tele-conference.[202]

The President and the Vice President

The President was seated in a classroom when, at 9:05, Andrew Card whispered to him: "A second plane hit the second tower. America is under attack." The President told us his instinct was to project calm, not to have the country see an excited reaction at a moment of crisis. The press was standing behind the children; he saw their phones and pagers start to ring. The President felt he should project strength and calm until he could better understand what was happening.[203]

The President remained in the classroom for another five to seven minutes, while the children continued reading. He then returned to a holding room shortly before 9:15, where he was briefed by staff and saw television coverage. He next spoke to Vice President Cheney, Dr. Rice, New York Governor George Pataki, and FBI Director Robert Mueller. He decided to make a brief statement from the school before leaving for the airport. The Secret Service told us they were anxious to move the President to a safer location, but did not think it imperative for him to run out the door.[204]

Between 9:15 and 9:30, the staff was busy arranging a return to Washington, while the President consulted his senior advisers about his remarks. No one in the traveling party had any information during this time that other aircraft were hijacked or missing. Staff was in contact with the White House Situation Room, but as far as we could determine, no one with the President was in contact with the Pentagon. The focus was on the President's statement to the nation. The only decision made during this time was to return to Washington.[205]

The President's motorcade departed at 9:35, and arrived at the airport between 9:42 and 9:45. During the ride the President learned about the attack on the Pentagon. He boarded the aircraft, asked the Secret Service about the safety of his family, and called the Vice President. According to notes of the call, at about 9:45 the President told the Vice President: "Sounds like we have a minor war going on here, I heard about the Pentagon. We're at war . . . some-body's going to pay."[206]

About this time, Card, the lead Secret Service agent, the President's military aide, and the pilot were conferring on a possible destination for

Air Force One. The Secret Service agent felt strongly that the situation in Washington was too unstable for the President to return there, and Card agreed. The President strongly wanted to return to Washington and only grudgingly agreed to go elsewhere. The issue was still undecided when the President conferred with the Vice President at about the time Air Force One was taking off. The Vice President recalled urging the President not to return to Washington. Air Force One departed at about 9:54 without any fixed destination. The objective was to get up in the air-as fast and as high as possible-and then decide where to go.[207]

At 9:33, the tower supervisor at Reagan National Airport picked up a hotline to the Secret Service and told the Service's operations center that "an aircraft [is] coming at you and not talking with us." This was the first specific report to the Secret Service of a direct threat to the White House. No move was made to evacuate the Vice President at this time. As the officer who took the call explained, "[I was] about to push the alert button when the tower advised that the aircraft was turning south and approaching Reagan National Airport."[208]

American 77 began turning south, away from the White House, at 9:34. It continued heading south for roughly a minute, before turning west and beginning to circle back. This news prompted the Secret Service to order the immediate evacuation of the Vice President just before 9:36. Agents propelled him out of his chair and told him he had to get to the bunker. The Vice President entered the underground tunnel leading to the shelter at 9:37.[209]

Once inside, Vice President Cheney and the agents paused in an area of the tunnel that had a secure phone, a bench, and television. The Vice President asked to speak to the President, but it took time for the call to be connected. He learned in the tunnel that the Pentagon had been hit, and he saw television coverage of smoke coming from the building.[210]

The Secret Service logged Mrs. Cheney's arrival at the White House at 9:52, and she joined her husband in the tunnel. According to contemporaneous notes, at 9:55 the Vice President was still on the phone with the President advising that three planes were missing and one had hit the Pentagon. We believe this is the same call in which the Vice President urged the President not to return to Washington. After the call ended, Mrs. Cheney and the Vice President moved from the tunnel to the shelter conference room.[211]

United 93 and the Shootdown Order

On the morning of 9/11, the President and Vice President stayed in contact not by an open line of communication but through a series of calls. The President told us he was frustrated with the poor communications that morning. He could not reach key officials, including Secretary Rumsfeld, for a period of time. The line to the White House shelter conference room-and the Vice President-kept cutting off.[212]

The Vice President remembered placing a call to the President just after entering the shelter conference room. There is conflicting evidence about when the Vice President arrived in the shelter conference room. We have concluded, from the available evidence, that the Vice President arrived in the room shortly before 10:00, perhaps at 9:58. The Vice President recalled being told, just after his arrival, that the Air Force was trying to establish a combat air patrol over Washington.[213]

The Vice President stated that he called the President to discuss the rules of engagement for the CAP. He recalled feeling that it did no good to establish the CAP unless the pilots had instructions on whether they were authorized to shoot if the plane would not divert. He said the President signed off on that concept. The President said he remembered such a conversation, and that it reminded him of when he had been an interceptor pilot. The President emphasized to us that he had authorized the shootdown of hijacked aircraft.[214]

The Vice President's military aide told us he believed the Vice President spoke to the President just after entering the conference room, but he did not hear what they said. Rice, who entered the room shortly after the Vice President and sat next to him, remembered hearing him inform the President, "Sir, the CAPs are up. Sir, they're going to want to know what to do." Then she recalled hearing him say, "Yes sir." She believed this conversation occurred a few minutes, perhaps five, after they entered the conference room.[215]

We believe this call would have taken place sometime before 10:10 to 10:15.

Among the sources that reflect other important events of that morning, there is no documentary evidence for this call, but the relevant sources are incomplete. Others nearby who were taking notes, such as the Vice President's chief of staff, Scooter Libby, who sat next to him, and Mrs.

Cheney, did not note a call between the President and Vice President immediately after the Vice President entered the conference room.[216]

At 10:02, the communicators in the shelter began receiving reports from the Secret Service of an inbound aircraft-presumably hijacked-heading toward Washington. That aircraft was United 93. The Secret Service was getting this information directly from the FAA. The FAA may have been tracking the progress of United 93 on a display that showed its projected path to Washington, not its actual radar return. Thus, the Secret Service was relying on projections and was not aware the plane was already down in Pennsylvania.[217]

At some time between 10:10 and 10:15, a military aide told the Vice President and others that the aircraft was 80 miles out. Vice President Cheney was asked for authority to engage the aircraft.[218] His reaction was described by Scooter Libby as quick and decisive, "in about the time it takes a batter to decide to swing." The Vice President authorized fighter aircraft to engage the inbound plane. He told us he based this authorization on his earlier conversation with the President. The military aide returned a few minutes later, probably between 10:12 and 10:18, and said the aircraft was 60 miles out. He again asked for authorization to engage. The Vice President again said yes.[219]

At the conference room table was White House Deputy Chief of Staff Joshua Bolten. Bolten watched the exchanges and, after what he called "a quiet moment," suggested that the Vice President get in touch with the President and confirm the engage order. Bolten told us he wanted to make sure the President was told that the Vice President had executed the order. He said he had not heard any prior discussion on the subject with the President.[220]

The Vice President was logged calling the President at 10:18 for a two-minute conversation that obtained the confirmation. On Air Force One, the President's press secretary was taking notes; Ari Fleischer recorded that at 10:20, the President told him that he had authorized a shootdown of aircraft if necessary.[221]

Minutes went by and word arrived of an aircraft down in Pennsylvania. Those in the shelter wondered if the aircraft had been shot down pursuant to this authorization.[222]

At approximately 10:30, the shelter started receiving reports of another hijacked plane, this time only 5 to 10 miles out. Believing they had only a minute or two, the Vice President again communicated the authorization to "engage or "take out" the aircraft. At 10:33, Hadley told the air threat conference call: "I need to get word to Dick Myers that our reports are there's an inbound aircraft flying low 5 miles out. The Vice President's guidance was we need to take them out."[223]

Once again, there was no immediate information about the fate of the inbound aircraft. In the apt description of one witness, "It drops below the radar screen and it's just continually hovering in your imagination; you don't know where it is or what happens to it." Eventually, the shelter received word that the alleged hijacker 5 miles away had been a medevac helicopter.[224]

Transmission of the Authorization from the White House to the Pilots

The NMCC learned of United 93's hijacking at about 10:03. At this time the FAA had no contact with the military at the level of national command. The NMCC learned about United 93 from the White House. It, in turn, was informed by the Secret Service's contacts with the FAA.[225]

NORAD had no information either. At 10:07, its representative on the air threat conference call stated that NORAD had "no indication of a hijack heading to DC at this time."[226]

Repeatedly between 10:14 and 10:19, a lieutenant colonel at the White House relayed to the NMCC that the Vice President had confirmed fighters were cleared to engage inbound aircraft if they could verify that the aircraft was hijacked.[227]

The commander of NORAD, General Ralph Eberhart, was en route to the NORAD operations center in Cheyenne Mountain, Colorado, when the shootdown order was communicated on the air threat conference call. He told us that by the time he arrived, the order had already been passed down NORAD's chain of command.[228]

It is not clear how the shootdown order was communicated within NORAD. But we know that at 10:31, General Larry Arnold instructed his staff to broadcast the following over a NORAD instant messaging system: "10:31 Vice president has cleared to us to intercept tracks of interest and shoot them down if they do not respond per [General Arnold]."[229]

In upstate New York, NEADS personnel first learned of the shootdown order from this message:

Floor Leadership: You need to read this.. . . The Region Commander has declared that we can shoot down aircraft that do not respond to our direction. Copy that?

Controllers: Copy that, sir.

Floor Leadership: So if you're trying to divert somebody and he won't divert-

Controllers: DO [Director of Operations] is saying no.

Floor Leadership: No? It came over the chat.. . .You got a conflict on that direction?

Controllers: Right now no, but-

Floor Leadership: Okay? Okay, you read that from the Vice President, right? Vice President has cleared. Vice President has cleared us to intercept traffic and shoot them down if they do not respond per [General Arnold].[230]

In interviews with us, NEADS personnel expressed considerable confusion over the nature and effect of the order.

The NEADS commander told us he did not pass along the order because he was unaware of its ramifications. Both the mission commander and the senior weapons director indicated they did not pass the order to the fighters circling Washington and New York because they were unsure how the pilots would, or should, proceed with this guidance. In short, while leaders in Washington believed that the fighters above them had been instructed to "take out" hostile aircraft, the only orders actually conveyed to the pilots were to "ID type and tail."[231]

In most cases, the chain of command authorizing the use of force runs from the president to the secretary of defense and from the secretary to the combatant commander. The President apparently spoke to Secretary Rumsfeld for the first time that morning shortly after 10:00. No one can recall the content of this conversation, but it was a brief call in which the subject of shootdown authority was not discussed.[232]

At 10:39, the Vice President updated the Secretary on the air threat conference:

Vice President: There's been at least three instances here where we've had reports of aircraft approaching Washington-a couple were confirmed hijack. And, pursuant to the President's instructions I gave authorization for them to be taken out. Hello?

SecDef: Yes, I understand. Who did you give that direction to?

Vice President: It was passed from here through the [operations] center at the White House, from the [shelter].

SecDef: OK, let me ask the question here. Has that directive been transmitted to the aircraft?

Vice President: Yes, it has.

SecDef: So we've got a couple of aircraft up there that have those instructions at this present time?

Vice President: That is correct. And it's my understanding they've already taken a couple of aircraft out.

SecDef: We can't confirm that. We're told that one aircraft is down but we do not have a pilot report that did it.[233]

As this exchange shows, Secretary Rumsfeld was not in the NMCC when the shootdown order was first conveyed. He went from the parking lot to his office (where he spoke to the President), then to the Executive Support Center, where he participated in the White House video teleconference. He moved to the NMCC shortly before 10:30, in order to join Vice Chairman Myers. Secretary Rumsfeld told us he was just gaining situational awareness when he spoke with the Vice President at 10:39. His primary concern was ensuring that the pilots had a clear understanding of their rules of engagement.[234]

The Vice President was mistaken in his belief that shootdown authorization had been passed to the pilots flying at NORAD's direction. By 10:45 there was, however, another set of fighters circling Washington that had entirely different rules of engagement. These fighters, part of the 113th Wing of the District of Columbia Air National Guard, launched out of Andrews Air Force Base in Maryland in response to information passed to them by the Secret Service. The first of the Andrews fighters was airborne at 10:38.[235]

General David Wherley-the commander of the 113th Wing-reached out to the Secret Service after hearing secondhand reports that it wanted fighters airborne. A Secret Service agent had a phone in each ear, one connected to Wherley and the other to a fellow agent at the White House, relaying instructions that the White House agent said he was getting from the Vice President. The guidance for Wherley was to send up the aircraft, with orders to protect the White House and take out any aircraft that threatened the Capitol. General Wherley translated this in military terms to flying "weapons free"-that is, the decision to shoot rests in the cockpit, or in this case in the cockpit of the lead pilot. He passed these instructions to the pilots that launched at 10:42 and afterward.[236]

Thus, while the fighter pilots under NORAD direction who had scrambled out of Langley never received any type of engagement order, the Andrews pilots were operating weapons free-a permissive rule of engagement. The President and the Vice President indicated to us they had not been aware that fighters had been scrambled out of Andrews, at the request of the Secret Service and outside the military chain of command.[237] There is no evidence that NORAD headquarters or military officials in the NMCC knew-during the morning of September 11-that the Andrews planes were airborne and operating under different rules of engagement.

What If?

NORAD officials have maintained consistently that had the passengers not caused United 93 to crash, the military would have prevented it from reaching Washington, D.C. That conclusion is based on a version of events that we now know is incorrect. The Langley fighters were not scrambled in response to United 93; NORAD did not have 47 minutes to intercept the flight; NORAD did not even know the plane was hijacked until after it had crashed. It is appropriate, therefore, to reconsider whether United 93 would have been intercepted.

Had it not crashed in Pennsylvania at 10:03, we estimate that United 93 could not have reached Washington any earlier than 10:13, and probably would have arrived before 10:23. There was only one set of fighters circling Washington during that time frame-the Langley F-16s. They were armed and under NORAD's control. After NEADS learned of the hijacking at 10:07, NORAD would have had from 6 to 16 minutes to locate the flight, receive authorization to shoot it down, and communicate the order to the pilots, who (in the same span) would have had to authenticate the order, intercept the flight, and execute the order.[238]

At that point in time, the Langley pilots did not know the threat they were facing, did not know where United 93 was located, and did not have shoot-down authorization.

First, the Langley pilots were never briefed about the reason they were scrambled. As the lead pilot explained, "I reverted to the Russian threat. ...I'm thinking cruise missile threat from the sea. You know you look down and see the Pentagon burning and I thought the bastards snuck one by us.. . . [Y]ou couldn't see any airplanes, and no one told us anything. "The pilots knew their mission was to divert aircraft, but did not know that the threat came from hijacked airliners.[239]

Second, NEADS did not have accurate information on the location of United 93. Presumably, FAA would have provided such information, but we do not know how long that would have taken, nor how long it would have taken NEADS to locate the target.

Third, NEADS needed orders to pass to the pilots. At 10:10, the pilots over Washington were emphatically told, "negative clearance to shoot." Shootdown authority was first communicated to NEADS at 10:31. It is possible that NORAD commanders would have ordered a shootdown in the absence of the authorization communicated by the Vice President, but given the gravity of the decision to shoot down a commercial airliner, and NORAD's caution that a mistake not be made, we view this possibility as unlikely.[240]

NORAD officials have maintained that they would have intercepted and shot down United 93. We are not so sure. We are sure that the nation owes a debt to the passengers of United 93. Their actions saved the lives of countless others, and may have saved either the Capitol or the White House from destruction.

The details of what happened on the morning of September 11 are complex, but they play out a simple theme. NORAD and the FAA were unprepared for the type of attacks launched against the United States on September 11, 2001. They struggled, under difficult circumstances, to improvise a homeland defense against an unprecedented challenge they had never before encountered and had never trained to meet.

At 10:02 that morning, an assistant to the mission crew commander at NORAD's Northeast Air Defense Sector in Rome, New York, was working with his colleagues on the floor of the command center. In a brief moment of reflection, he was recorded remarking that "This is a new type of war."[241]

He was, and is, right. But the conflict did not begin on 9/11. It had been publicly declared years earlier, most notably in a declaration faxed early in 1998 to an Arabic-language newspaper in London. Few Americans had noticed it. The fax had been sent from thousands of miles away by the followers of a Saudi exile gathered in one of the most remote and impoverished countries on earth.

ACKNOWLEDGMENTS

Snow Day was started in 2017 as a book about technology transforming how security set strategy, policy, and processes. The initial focus was on customized and COTS technologies for better analysis and communication to better identify probable risks and manage disruptive situations. During many visits with technology companies and enterprise security programs, the shift to analyzing and managing threats before they materialized became a realistic and affordable posture. At the same time, the C-suite understanding of security's value to the business sank in. The original book focused on bringing ideas about shifting from the manual and reactive security programs that failed to helping risk management get ahead of and be prepared for both predictable and unanticipated events.

As new technology-centric solutions including robotics, drones, and even smartphones became available and affordable options for security, adoption was low. Most security organizations sat in a reactive posture relying on the long used manual processes. When I returned to speaking with the top tier of security leaders, I observed how they were employing technology to transform their programs by gathering information for analysis, synthesis, and action against potential threats.

The best were using technology to stop disruption and provide resilience. They were communicating with the business units to understand their goals and support their success. And they became highly recognized by the C-suite as a key component of enterprise success.

As the COVID-19 pandemic blindsided many businesses, those with crisis management programs in place were best positioned to leverage their infrastructure and respond by both keeping the business open and keeping people safe.

Similar to Chelsey "Sully" Sullenberger's quote after safely landing on the Hudson River, who said,

> *One way of looking at this might be that for 42 years, I've been making small, regular deposits in this bank of experience, education and training. And on January 15 the balance was sufficient so that I could make a very large withdrawal.*

Businesses were making an investment in their own futures toward having the people, processes, and technology in place, trained and ready to handle a crisis. And there are crises arising constantly for security teams.

During my time leading the Security 500 program, many chief security officers presented the economic case for security spend. During his tenure as the chief security officer at Dell, John McClurg set the security mission to "Enable and Assure Business," which I immediately "borrowed" as the tagline for the new business publication.

I am indebted to John, whose friendship and brilliance helped build the Security 500 and *Security* magazine to unimagined success. Thank you for the foreword, which truly summarizes *Snow Day*'s theme and voice.

Before there was a business publication for the security profession, David Shepherd participated in a focus group to set the editorial vision. His simple statement about 9/11, "Overnight our jobs went from cutting cost to saving lives," was seminal in our thinking. His company is Readiness Resource Group, and their customers rely on them for services ensuring preparedness, operational readiness, and organizational resilience. Dave's insights and voice are weaved into *Snow Day*'s theme.

When I met Maureen Rush, I proposed an interview about the University of Pennsylvania's public safety program and police department. She brought her rolodex, and that story grew to include many of the partners that drove Penn's successful programs from the city, manned guard services company, technology integrator, and other Penn department leaders. With Maureen, success truly lies in relationships. I have been blessed with her friendship for many years. A solid business mind and security expert, her enthusiastic advice has helped shape simple ideas into reality. *Snow Day* was just one of the many where her expertise, experience, and care contributed tremendously to the overall work. Far beyond the University of Pennsylvania campus, Maureen's influence and thought has helped both the city of Philadelphia and universities worldwide improve the lives of those they are entrusted to care for.

I first met Kenneth Damstrom when he was the chief security officer at Lehman Brothers and asked him, "What do you read to do your job?" He answered, "The Wall Street Journal," but wanted a business magazine. That led to the Business Week design for Security and a longtime friendship. He most recently retired as managing director and chief security officer at Goldman Sachs after a stellar career ensuring and enabling the bank's business. As a frequent keynote speaker at my events and interview subject, his insights and thoughtful approach to leadership, cross-functional partnerships, and working to facilitate business goals for his internal customers resonates throughout the profession today.

There is no better sounding board than Lynn Mattice because he encourages what is right and quickly kills what is wrong. Lynn generously shared his knowledge, time, and rolodex for *Snow Day*. Lynn's expertise as a former security and business executive promotes the decision-making and communications that define good leadership. No matter what your review of the book is, it is much better than it would have been without Lynn's guidance.

Among the many special technology back lot tours I was privileged to experience, Mike Howard, while chief security officer at Microsoft, arranged a demonstration of their Virtual Security Operations Center. It was a significant motivator for starting this book. While writing his own book (*The Art of Ronin Leadership: Strategy, Execution, Sustained Success*), he took the time to help steer and edit *Snow Day*. Mike was among the first to bring CIOs, CISOs, financial and business leaders from Microsoft to security industry media events educating other leaders on how to make the business case through the business leader's lens.

John O'Connor was at Fidelity Investments and among the first "business executives that happened to manage the security function" when we met. His business-minded focus on communicating security's value in relation to the business and the customer tied directly to managing risk and enduring resilience. He was among the few to read the first chapter and encourage my writing efforts. His focus on metrics and active participation with the Security 500 benchmarking program advanced the project and increased its value for members.

Meeting Jack Briggs was a mix of magic and luck. Asked to host a panel at a NYC Conference, I decided to test *Snow Day* and invited my friend Marlon Lynch, vice president of Public Safety for NYU at the time. We discussed *Snow Day*, and he assured me that I really wanted Jack. He was right. Jack's contribution to that panel and *Snow Day* is irreplaceable as he is unique in the thinking, leadership, and experience required in crisis management. His brilliance and patience during the writing are greatly appreciated.

The first time I saw Jeff Miller was on the news following the horrible shooting at the West Nickel Mines School in Pennsylvania's Amish Country killing five children. Jeff was the commissioner of the Pennsylvania State Police and stood tall during those difficult press briefings. We met when he became the chief security officer for the National Football League and was active in many of my programs, including being recognized as one of the Most Influential People in Security. He has been gracious in providing the back lot tour of the Kansas City Chief's security and safety programs during COVID-19 and finding the time for interviews during the NFL playoffs and Super Bowl. He continues to stand tall in all he does.

Dan Sauvageau filled John O'Connor's shoes at Fidelity Investments as CSO and led the program to new heights before retiring. It was fitting that I asked him to read the *Snow Day* manuscript and get his advice. His contributions in the chapter "A Different Kind of Crisis" are insightful for crisis management program leaders and the essential need to successfully communicate value and to the C-suite.

Joe Oliveraz is among the most transformative leaders in the security and risk profession. His approach is to enable business by figuring it out and saying yes to his internal customers. He is a creator of best practices that the profession should learn from and follow, and I hope the interview captured that appropriately.

Brian Tuskan had the unenviable task of stepping into Mike Howard's shoes as chief security officer at Microsoft. Prior to his promotion, his forward thinking about security technology and information analysis was central to his work, I continue to benefit from his clear thinking about risk management and resilience programs. He has successfully set his own agenda as a leader and brought that forward in our interview.

Jack Sullivan's insights and focus on security's measurable contribution to business is unparalleled. During our friendship, he has been a constant resource about both risk management and the security profession. His contribution to *Snow Day* goes far beyond the published interview and contributed to the completed work.

While Mark Landry's name does not appear in *Snow Day*, his valuable thinking does. His drive to leverage technology that actually works and brings benefits to the business and the security program is constant and has paid off well for his company, FedEx.

George McCloskey's friendship and encouragement motivated me to dust off the first chapters and complete the book during the pandemic. His direction on key aspects of *Snow Day* were incredibly helpful. His transformative thinking about security's economic value to achieving business goals has contributed greatly to the profession.

My thanks to Dr. Park Dietz for the time and energy he put into *Snow Day*. He clearly and directly opened my eyes, as he will the readers, about the longer-term consequences and costs COVID-19 will hold. He brought a necessary weight and view to the crisis management discussion.

Steve Bernard greeted me warmly when I first visited Sony Pictures for an interview. As the chief security officer, he managed through many crises, including the Fukushima earthquake and the North Korean "Guardians of Peace" cyberattack. My thanks to him for those enjoyable days touring the studio and learning from him.

Dr. Lou Marciani invited me to volunteer as an advisor to the National Center for Spectator Sports Safety & Security and recently to the Innovation Institute for Fan Experience. The former as a response to event safety after 9/11 and the latter to return fans to events safely after COVID-19. His work is invaluable to anyone who attends events, from the high school to professional level, including sports and concerts. Thankfully, he has become my advisor and an important voice in my work.

My friend Eric Moe is among the elite writers and directors in the LA entertainment business. His reading and editing of *Snow Day* made it more readable. His advice to make it "shorter, even shorter than that" was a kind gesture to the reader.

My appreciation and thanks to friends who helped form my thinking by giving me access to new technologies, security advancements, and insights into how crisis management programs, teams, and decisions are really made. Dave Komendat at Boeing; Bonnie Michelman at Massachusetts General Hospital, Michael Sher at GroupDoLists; Bud Broomhead at Viakoo; Dr. Travis Deyle at Cobalt Robotics; and David Meredith at Everbridge for contributing in unique and vital ways to the writing of *Snow Day*.

BIOGRAPHIES

Stevan Bernard

Stevan Bernard is the Chief Executive Officer of Bernard Global, LLC which he founded in May 2018 capping a diverse career that has spanned 50 years, working and living in over 50 countries (6 Continents) and serving in leading roles in both government and the private sector. Bernard Global's scope of services includes advising senior-management on all facets of global protection services; an emphasis on cyber security; creating and conducting awareness programs; executive recruiting; BCP, partnering with the FBI and Department of State to enhance awareness and build trust. For nearly 17 years he led Sony Pictures Entertainment's global protection services with responsibility for the CSO/CISO function, investigations and forensics, physical security, BCP, environment, medical, major events and protection, employee health and safety. Prior to this he worked in high-tech, energy and law-enforcement. His service in the US Army included a tour in Vietnam where he was awarded the Bronze Star. He is a Certified Fraud Examiner, with degrees in Criminal Justice and Psychology. He graduated from the 125th Session of the FBI National Academy @Quantico.

Jack Briggs

Major General Briggs served in the United States Air Force with over 31 years in a variety of senior leadership roles. Most recently he was responsible for the defense of North America, support to all federal agencies and state governments during civil operations including natural and man-made disasters, and coordinating nation to nation security cooperation operations in North America. His unique background includes extensive international and domestic experience at all levels with assignments in England, Hungary, Italy, Germany, the Azores (Portugal), Belgium, Canada and the United States. He has served multiple combat tours as a fighter pilot and staff officer and as commander of the largest operational flying command in Afghanistan during the surge in operations from 2010-2011.

As the Director of Operations for the U.S. Northern Command from 2014-2017 at Peterson Air Force Base in Colorado, Major General Briggs directed all US Armed Forces ground, air, maritime, operations from the Arctic Circle to the Mexico-Guatemala border. Primary operations officer responsible for executing North American Homeland Defense and Defense Support to Civil Authorities. Managed day to day affairs of 11 subject matter expert driven lines of operation for national strategy and operational execution including support to the President of the United States, Ballistic Missile Defense, Cyber Protection, response to natural disasters such as wildfires, floods, and hurricanes. Developed extensive relationships with Centers for Disease Control, National Institutes of Health, Department of Homeland Security, Nuclear Regulatory Commission, Drug Enforcement Agency, Department of Energy, and Environmental Protection Agency.

As Vice Commander for the 1st Air Force from 2013-2014 at Tyndall Air Force Base in Florida, Brigadier General Briggs led all air operations in support of national interests in the North America area of responsibility. Primarily responsible for the day-to-day air operations for Homeland Defense, Defense Support to Civilian Agencies and Theater Security Cooperation with Mexico and the Bahamas. Responsible for the welfare and development of over 600 military and civilian members.

Serving as Deputy Commander, Canadian NORAD Region from 2011-2013 in Winnipeg, Canada with the rank of Brigadier General, he led North American Aerospace Defense operations in the Canadian region. Directed the day-to-day missions for 10 Canadian Air Wings including Homeland Defense, Defense Support to Civilian Agencies. Served as the senior US military officer assigned to Canada. Decorated by the Governor General of Canada with the Meritorious Service Medal.

As a Distinguished Graduate of the United States Air Force Academy and the Wright Brothers Award winner for Outstanding Leadership at Air War College, Major General Briggs was also the first US Military officer to attend a graduate school in the Republic of Hungary as an Olmsted Scholar.

After his service in the United States Air Force, he led Vice President,

166

Global Resiliency and Security at New York University responsible for the University's Emergency Management and Continuity, a Global Security Operations Center, a Communications Center, Fire Life Safety, Global Academic Center Security Operations, and Security Technology for NYU's 15 campuses in 11 countries for over 70,000 students, faculty, and administration. He led NYU's COVID-19 response as a change agent instituting processes and procedures to build an agile and effective planning, mitigation, response, and recovery architecture to ensure readiness for the missions of teaching, research, and public service.

During 2020, Jack became President and CEO of the Springs Rescue Mission, a large gospel rescue mission with over $20 million in assets and overseeing programs that provide housing, health and work. In 2020, Springs Rescue Mission provided over 200,000 meals, 116,000 nights of shelter for guests and placed 265 people in permanent housing. In addition, 1,600 guests received medical assistance and 20,000 hours of job skills training. Springs Rescue Mission is recognized by Charity Navigator as a top-ranked Four-Star Charity.

Park Dietz

Park Dietz, MD, MPH, PhD, is Clinical Professor of Psychiatry at the UCLA David Geffen School of Medicine and founder and president of both Threat Assessment Group, Inc., and Park Dietz & Associates, Inc., of Newport Beach, CA. Educated at Cornell, Johns Hopkins, and the University of Pennsylvania, he served as Assistant Professor of Psychiatry at Harvard Medical School, and served as Professor of Law and Professor of Behavioral Medicine and Psychiatry at the University of Virginia. He often appears as an expert witness in high-profile trials and has been named one of the 10 most famous psychiatrists in history by biography. com. He created the specialty of workplace violence prevention and has been named one of the "Top 25 Most Influential People in the Security Industry" by Security magazine.

Dr. Myles Druckman

Dr. Myles Druckman is the Group Medical Director for Health Innovation and leads the development and management of innovative solutions that protect people and their institutions from global health threats. His work is making the world safer and healthier - one organization at a time.

He is a leader in International Corporate Health, Medical Risk Management, Pandemic Preparedness, and planning for and management of global health incidents. Consults to many of the world's top organizations. Published academic author on global health risks, and frequent speaker and regular expert resource for TV and print media.

He serves as Co-Chairman of the International Corporate Health Leadership Council (ICHLC).

Dr. Druckman has extensive international healthcare experience including

- Regional Medical Director based in Beijing (1996-2001) - developed 4 western medical facilities, 3 alarm centers and over 25 remote site medical operations.
- Deputy Chairman and Chief Medical Officer of American Medical Centers in Moscow (1991-1996).
- Set up the first western medical facilities in the former Soviet Union - Moscow, St. Petersburg, Kiev.

He is a "Global Leader of Tomorrow" alumni at the World Economic Forum, and board member of WaterAid.

His specialties include international healthcare expertise, experience consulting to major fortune 500 companies, leading expert in Pandemic Preparedness, expertise in managing global emergencies.

George McCloskey

George has a background of success as an experienced CSO that has built employee focused security and safety programs that protect organizations from systemic and aggregated risk. His focus is on people first, and he scales to the culture to build sensible solutions with an emphasis on resiliency, operational safety and security, cyber security, executive protective services, travel safety & global mobility, supply chain, business continuity and resiliency, and global real estate. He has demonstrated success in the creation and implementation of effective security and life safety programs and strategies at some of the most innovative, and creative organizations over many culturally and geographically diverse regions of the world.

Jeffrey Miller

Responsible for developing and managing all safety and security plans and programs for all facets of the Kansas City Chiefs football Club. This includes 24/7 facility security, event day safety, security and traffic operations, team security and ownership security.

As Owner of Jeffrey Miller Consulting, LLC, he provides comprehensive security consulting services focused on counterterrorism and risk mitigation measures designed to help clients protect their patrons, venues and events. With years of experience in securing major events both within and outside the US, he brings real-world knowledge to bear in devising practical solutions to complex security challenges. His clients include professional sports teams in the US and Europe, colleges and universities in all of the major conferences, Bowl games, police departments, and concert promoters and venues.

Previously served as Commissioner of the 9th largest police organization in the U.S. with 6400 enlisted and civilian personnel and a budget of over three quarters of a billion dollars. Was empowered by statute to assist the Governor in enforcing the law by exercising command and fiscal authority over all state police operations in 67 counties of the Commonwealth of Pennsylvania.

As Chief Security Officer for the NFL, led and supervised all facets of security for the NFL to include all investigative programs and services, event security (including Super Bowl and International Series), game integrity program, executive protection, fan conduct initiative and stadium security program. This role also coordinates emergency and business continuity planning for the NFL, facility security for all NFL business locations as well as ongoing department liaison with federal and state authorities at the senior level.

Cary Monbarren

Global Manager of Physical Security, Safety & Business Resilence

Mr. Monbarren joined Slack in May 2018 and leads the company's global security, safety and business resilience programs. In this role he leads the administrative, management and technology programs including leading crisis management team planning, training and communications.

He is a service-focused business leader with tactical and technical expertise including a solid background and extensive knowledge in safety and security management, policy and procedures. He is highly proficient in creating, driving and implementing high-level security plans to enhance security/protection of personnel, property and territory.

He began his career as an infantryman in the United States Marine Corps. After 12 years of packing a machine gun around the world he was selected for recruiting duty in Montana. He served overseas in support of Operation Iraqi Freedom, and upon his return enrolled at the University of Montana and completed a bachelor's degree in Business Administration. An assignment to a Weapons of Mass Destruction response team piqued his interest in domestic operations and security; leading him enroll in the Master of Science in Security Administration (MSSA) at Southwestern College, Kansas.

Prior to joining Slack, Mr. Monbarren managed data center security at Facebook and was a senior trainer for nuclear security at Duke Energy.

Joe Olivarez

- Vice President, Operational Center of Excellence & CSO at Jacobs
- A strategic business and executive leader with an MBA and over 30 years of security practitioner experience overseeing and/or consulting to Fortune 500 and government enterprise security programs. Recognized as a strategic planner and visionary with highly effective skills in executing business plans. Creator of strategic partnerships with key stakeholders and a consensus builder with an ability to move the business forward through education, influence and planning of risk management activities.
- He is a member of the Global Board of Directors ASIS International and an Advisory Board member of the Overseas Advisory Security Council.

Maureen S Rush, M.S., CPP

Maureen S. Rush is the Vice President for Public Safety and Superintendent of the Penn Police Department. Ms. Rush joined the

Division of Public Safety in 1994 as the Director of Victim Support & Special Services. Ms. Rush then served as the Chief of the Penn Police Department from 1996 through 2000. She was appointed Vice President for Public Safety at the University of Pennsylvania in 2000. As the CEO of the agency her duties include directing the tactical and strategic focus of the Division of Public Safety and all aspects of Law Enforcement, Safety and Security Technology, and Emergency Preparedness. She is responsible for managing a budget of over $27 million dollars and encompassing eight departments totaling 181 Penn employees. The departments include: The Office of the Vice President, the University of Pennsylvania Police Department, Security Technology, Emergency Communications, Fire & Emergency Services, Special Services, Security Services and Finance & Administration. The Division of Public Safety also employs approximately 550 AlliedBarton contract security officers to secure buildings, student residences and supplement the Penn Police Department on street patrol within the Penn Police patrol jurisdiction. The Division of Public Safety is responsible for all Emergency Preparedness and Crisis Planning for the University.

During her tenure, the Penn's Police Department evolved into a model campus law enforcement agency, continually meeting the challenges faced by an urban university, while at the same time strengthening its relationships with the Penn and West Philadelphia communities, and with the City of Philadelphia. With 121 police officers, the Penn Police Department is the largest private police department in the state of Pennsylvania. In March 2001, the Penn Police Department was awarded national accreditation from the Commission on Accreditation for Law Enforcement Agencies, Inc. (CALEA), becoming the first nationally accredited campus police agency within the Commonwealth of Pennsylvania. The Penn Police Department remains accredited through CALEA, most recently being awarded ADVANCED Reaccreditation in April 2016. CALEA administers a rigorous accreditation process whereby law enforcement agencies must adhere to over 440 standards, codes and state-of-the-art practices.

Prior to coming to the University of Pennsylvania, Ms. Rush had a distinguished eighteen-year law enforcement career with the Philadelphia Police Department from 1976 through 1994. Ms. Rush served in various positions, namely: the Patrol Division, the Anti-Crime Unit, the Traffic Division, the Narcotics Unit, and the Training Bureau. In 1976, Ms. Rush was one of the first 100 women police officers hired to serve the City of

Philadelphia on "street patrol" in a pilot program directed by the United States Department of Justice. Women now comprise twenty-five percent of the Philadelphia Police Department, with approximately 1,650 officers, because of that successful pilot program.

Ms. Rush has extensive knowledge of urban law enforcement and the interaction between a college campus and the community, and lectures nationally on this subject. The Division of Public Safety has become a national model for its successful Private/Public venture. Ms. Rush serves on numerous committees and task forces within the city and state, which address these key interests. In 1999, she served as a member of the City of Philadelphia's Public Safety Transition Team, and continues to work closely with numerous City of Philadelphia agencies, most importantly the Philadelphia Police & Fire Departments. In 2002, Ms. Rush served on Governor Rendell's Pennsylvania Homeland Security Transition Team. In November 2015, Ms. Rush was appointed co-chair to Mayor-Elect Jim Kenney's Public Safety Policy transition team. Ms. Rush currently serves on the following Boards: President of the Philadelphia Police Foundation Board; Vice President of the University City Associates; Vice Chairman of the Philadelphia Police Athletic League Board; Secretary of the University City District; United Way of Southeastern Pennsylvania; The Citizen's Crime Commission; and Penn Vet Working Dog Center Advisory Board. Additionally, Ms. Rush serves on numerous committees within the University of Pennsylvania, such as the President's Senior Planning Group and, University Council, as well as the Task Force on Student Psychological Health and Welfare, the Commission on Student Safety, Alcohol and Campus Life and the Task Force on a Safe and Responsible Campus Community.

Ms. Rush is a Fellow with the University of Pennsylvania's Fox Leadership Program within the School of Arts and Sciences.

Since 2003 Ms. Rush has served as the Co-Chair for the University of Pennsylvania's Annual Workplace Giving "Penn's Way Campaign," which raised over $1,600,000 during the COVID-19 Pandemic with many faculty and staff working remotely. The Campaign works with the United Way of Southeastern Pennsylvania, the Center for Responsible Funding and Penn Medicine in providing funding for non-profit organizations serving the Philadelphia region.

Ms. Rush received numerous commendations from the Philadelphia Police Department and has received awards from the Chapel of the Four

Chaplains, the Bryn Mawr Women's Business Association, the Girl Scouts of Southeastern Pennsylvania's Take the Lead award, and the Black Men at Penn School of Social Work, Inc.

Under Ms. Rush's leadership, the University of Pennsylvania's Division of Public Safety was recognized as the number one institution in the Higher Education vertical market, as ranked by Security Magazine's Security 500 Survey for 10 years in a row.

Ms. Rush holds a M.S. degree from the University of Pennsylvania in Organizational Dynamics. She has also completed the John F. Kennedy School of Government, the Northwestern School of Staff & Command and the FBI's Law Enforcement Executive Development Program. In 2004, Ms. Rush completed a year-long program with Philadelphia Leadership, Inc. a regional leadership think tank and during the same year, earned a Certified Protection Professional (CPP) certification from the American Society for Industrial Security (ASIS) International Professional Certification Board. In 2009 Ms. Rush completed a Security Executive certification program sponsored by the University of Pennsylvania's Wharton School and the American Society for Industrial Security (ASIS).

Ms. Rush received Security Magazine's "Most Influential People in Security" honor in September 2015. Ms. Rush received the Egon Bittner Award for Excellence in Leadership of a CALEA Accredited Law Enforcement Agency for 15 consecutive years in April 2016.

Dan Sauvageau

Dan is currently a member of the faculty with the Security Executive Council (SEC) a leading global security & risk consultancy firm. He joined the SEC in September 2019 following his retirement from Fidelity Investments after a 28-year career with the Company. At Fidelity, he served in a variety of senior security roles including as its Chief Security Officer (CSO) for 5 years. While CSO, he was directly responsible for the strategic direction and leadership of a 300+ person global proprietary team of security professionals, comprised of Operations, Investigations, Due Diligence and Background Vetting functions providing a comprehensive array of security, safety, and investigative services for 43,000 global employees with a $50M operating and capital expense budget. While a member of the Senior Security Leadership team and as CSO, Fidelity Corporate Security was awarded 1st place awards from Security Management magazine, on four separate occasions, for having the best security program in the entire U.S. Financial Services sector.

Prior to joining Fidelity Investments, Dan spent five years managing security programs for multi-million dollar classified Department of Defense projects at Sanders Associates, a Lockheed Corp. He provided a variety of asset protection, training, audit and security services for people and programs as well as specialized security plans and programs to safeguard classified Department of Defense information.

Dan holds a BA degree in Criminal Justice from St. Anselm College and an MBA from Rivier University. He is a board-Certified Protection Professional (CPP) with the American Society of Industrial Security (ASIS). Dan serves as a member of Rivier University's Board of Trustees and in August of 2019, he joined the Security Executive Council as an Emeritus Faculty Member.

Jack Sullivan

John L. Sullivan has been the Chief Security Officer (CSO) of Boston Scientific (BSC) since 2017. Prior to joining BSC, John was the CSO of Starbucks for four years. John spent 10 years in the US Marines prior to becoming a Special Agent with a US Government agency. John left the government to earn a master's degree in Government at Harvard University where he earned the Dean's List Award for Academic Achievement. John also has an MBA from the Sloan School of Management at the Massachusetts Institute of Technology. He is a board advisor to tech startups in Boston, New York, Washington D.C., Tel Aviv and Seattle. In addition to his advisory roles with these startups, he is a Board Advisor to several Venture Capital firms in Boston, New York, San Francisco and Tel Aviv. He resides on the South Shore of Massachusetts with his wife and two young daughters.

Brian Tuskan

Brian Tuskan has over 30 years of experience in law enforcement and the private security sector. He is currently the Sr. Director, Chief Security Officer for Microsoft's Global Security Operations in the Real Estate & Security Organization. Brian's team is responsible for the physical security of all of Microsoft's global footprint: Security Operations, Investigations, Threat Management, High-Value Assets, Intelligence, Virtual Security

Operations Centers, Executive Protection, Risk & Enterprise Resiliency, Event Risk Management, & Background Screening.

Brian's team provides insight and requirements for Microsoft's Digital Transformation of the physical security environments of the corporation. The teams are vital contributors to the technology development of Microsoft's global security's Virtual Security Operations Center (VSOC). The VSOC will be the SOC of the future leveraging the intelligent cloud, intelligent edge, AI, robotics, and 3D mixed reality to manage global life-safety security operations.

As a public servant, Brian spent over 12 years in law enforcement with the City of Redmond Police (Washington) and the Honolulu Police Department. During his distinguished law enforcement career, he worked as a patrol officer, ATV specialized unit, SWAT tactical team member, criminal intelligence and analysis, undercover narcotics detective, major crimes detective, and officer-in-charge. Brian was named one of The Most Influential People in Security 2017.

He founded Cop to Corporate, which helps law enforcement professionals plan their transition to the private sector. Brian has a Criminal Justice degree from Wayland Baptist University, is a graduate of the University of Washington (Foster School of Business, EDP) and received an Executive Leadership Certificate from Georgetown University. Brian sits on the Microsoft Worldwide Public Safety and Justice Advisory Council, is an Advisory Board Member of Secure Strategy Group, and served on the ASIS Leadership & Management Practices Council.

BIBLIOGRAPHY

"The 9/11 Commission Report." Accessed May 12, 2021. https://www.
govinfo.gov/features/911-commission-report.

"9/11 Tape Has Late Change On Evacuation (Published 2004)." The New
York Times - Breaking News, US News, World News and Videos.
Last modified May 17, 2004. https://www.nytimes.com/2004/05/17/
nyregion/9-11-tape-has-late-change-on-evacuation.html.

ABC News. "How Will New York Keep Out a Rising Sea?" ABC News.
Last modified November 14, 2012. https://abcnews.go.com/US/
york-rising-sea/story?id=17720064.

Beaton, Andrew, and Louise Radnofsky. "The NFL's Covid-19 Finding That
Saved the Season." WSJ. Last modified January 31, 2021. https://
www.wsj.com/articles/super-bowl-nfl-covid-cdc-11612104460.

Beaton, Andrew, and Louise Radnofsky. "The NFL's Covid-19 Finding That
Saved the Season." WSJ. Last modified January 31, 2021. https://
www.wsj.com/articles/super-bowl-nfl-covid-cdc-11612104460.

"The Black Swan." Goodreads | Meet Your Next Favorite Book. Accessed
May 12, 2021. https://www.goodreads.com/book/show/242472.
The_Black_Swan.

Chaturvedi, Ayush. "Of Black Swans and Grey Rhinos." The Wisdom Project. Last modified March 15, 2020. https://wisdomproject. substack.com/p/of-black-swans-and-grey-rhinos.

"Coronavirus Vaccine Development: from SARS and MERS to COVID-19." Journal of Biomedical Science. Accessed May 12, 2021. https://jbiomedsci.biomedcentral.com/articles/10.1186/ s12929-020-00695-2.

"COVID-19 Cases, Deaths, and Trends in the US | CDC COVID Data Tracker." Centers for Disease Control and Prevention. Last modified March 28, 2020. https://covid.cdc.gov/covid-data-tracker/#trends_ dailytrendsdeaths.

"The Definition of Digital Transformation." Brian Solis. Last modified August 25, 2019. https://www.briansolis.com/2017/01/ definition-of-digital-transformation/.

"Delay Meant Death on 9/11." USA TODAY: Latest World and US News - USATODAY.com. Last modified September 3, 2002. https:// usatoday30.usatoday.com/news/sept11/2002-09-02-choices-usat_ x.htm.

Forbes. Accessed May 12, 2021. https://www.forbes.com/sites/ edwardsegal/2021/03/04/heres-the-latest-crisis-management-lesson -from-the-capitol-riot-command-chains-matter/?sh=5ae49d7f2cc1.

"Gray Rhino – Michele Wucker's Website." Michele Wucker's Website – Michele Wucker's Website. Accessed May 12, 2021. https://www. wucker.com/tag/gray-rhino/.

"The Gray Rhino." Goodreads | Meet Your Next Favorite Book. Accessed May 12, 2021. https://www.goodreads.com/book/ show/23848071-the-gray-rhino.

Harder, Amy. "Coronavirus and Climate Change Are Obvious Risks We Ignore." Axios. Last modified March 9, 2020. https://www.axios.

com/coronavirus-climate-change-risks-bc81ec96-ca03-4af7-867f-2aac2648b2d5.html.

"How News Media is Describing the Incident at the U.S. Capitol." Visual Capitalist. Last modified January 16, 2021. https://www.visualcapitalist.com/how-news-media-is-describing-the-incident-at-the-u-s-capitol/.

Kiley, Sam, and Ingrid Formanek and Ivana KottasováVideo by Alex Platt. "In the Congo Rainforest, the Doctor Who Discovered Ebola Warns of Deadly Viruses Yet to Come." CNN. Last modified December 24, 2020. https://www.cnn.com/2020/12/22/africa/drc-forest-new-virus-intl/index.html.

"Los Angeles and New York Differ in Their Responses to a Terrorism Threat (Published 2015)." The New York Times - Breaking News, US News, World News and Videos. Last modified December 16, 2015. https://www.nytimes.com/2015/12/16/us/los-angeles-schools-bomb-threat.html.

"Maturing Your Organization's Approach to Work-from-Home: A Focus on Wellness and Productivity." Critical Event Management, Keep Your People Safe & Operations Running. Accessed May 12, 2021. https://go.everbridge.com/go.everbridge.com/go.everbridge.com/go.everbridge.com/go.everbridge.com/wellness-and-productivity-whitepaper-reg-page.html.

Maurer, Roy. "Study Finds Productivity Not Deterred by Shift to Remote Work." SHRM. Last modified September 16, 2020. https://www.shrm.org/hr-today/news/hr-news/Pages/Study-Productivity-Shift-Remote-Work-COVID-Coronavirus.aspx.

"The Mental Health Pandemic Calls for a Strategic Initiative That Emphasizes Integrative Health Care." Psychiatric Times. Last modified October 27, 2020. https://www.psychiatrictimes.com/view/mental-health-pandemic-calls-strategic-initiative-that-emphasizes-integrative-health-care.

"Microsoft - Responding to COVID-19." Responding to COVID-19 Together. Last modified July 23, 2020. https://news.microsoft.com/covid-19-response/.

"Microsoft." Cybersecurity Excellence Awards. Last modified February 25, 2019. https://cybersecurity-excellence-awards.com/candidates/microsoft/.

"Nursing Home Linked to 37 Coronavirus Deaths Faces Fine of $600,000." The New York Times - Breaking News, World News & Multimedia. Last modified April 2, 2020. https://www.nytimes.com/2020/04/02/us/virus-kirkland-life-care-nursing-home.html.

"The Only Plane in the Sky." Garrett M. Graff. Last modified May 22, 2019. https://www.garrettgraff.com/books/the-only-plane-in-the-sky/.

Opinion by Scott Hadland. "Opinion: The Other Health Crisis the Stimulus Package Will Help." CNN. Last modified March 10, 2021. https://www.cnn.com/2021/03/10/opinions/drug-addiction-overdose-crisis-covid-relief-bill-hadland/index.html.

"Rising Currents: Projects for New York's Waterfront | MoMA." The Museum of Modern Art. Accessed May 12, 2021. https://www.moma.org/calendar/exhibitions/1028.

"Road to Nowhere: Minor Snowstorm Brings Atlanta to Standstill." CBS News - Breaking News, 24/7 Live Streaming News & Top Stories. Last modified January 30, 2014. https://www.cbsnews.com/news/atlanta-other-parts-of-south-paralyzed-by-ice-snowstorm/.

"State-Specific Costs of Motor Vehicle Crash Deaths." Centers for Disease Control and Prevention. Last modified November 6, 2020. https://www.cdc.gov/transportationsafety/statecosts/index.html.

"What Impact Have Terrorist Attacks Had on the Insurance Industry?" Investopedia. Accessed May 12, 2021. https://www.investopedia.com/ask/answers/050115/what-impact-have-terrorist-attacks-had-insurance-industry.asp.

CPSIA information can be obtained
at www.ICGtesting.com
Printed in the USA
LVHW090540010821
694197LV00003B/35/J

9 781664 178816